Argumentation Strategies in the Classroom

Chrysi Rapanta
Universidade Nova de Lisboa, Portugal

Series in Education

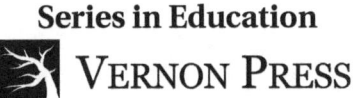

Copyright © 2019 Vernon Press, an imprint of Vernon Art and Science Inc, on behalf of the author.

All rights reserved. No part of this publication may be reproduced, stored in a retrieval system, or transmitted in any form or by any means, electronic, mechanical, photocopying, recording, or otherwise, without the prior permission of Vernon Art and Science Inc.

www.vernonpress.com

In the Americas:
Vernon Press
1000 N West Street,
Suite 1200, Wilmington,
Delaware 19801
United States

In the rest of the world:
Vernon Press
C/Sancti Espiritu 17,
Malaga, 29006
Spain

Series in Education

Library of Congress Control Number: 2018966499

ISBN: 978-1-62273-690-4

Also available:

Hardback: 978-1-62273-313-2

E-book: 978-1-62273-579-2

Cover design by Vernon Press.

Cover image designed by Freepik

Product and company names mentioned in this work are the trademarks of their respective owners. While every care has been taken in preparing this work, neither the authors nor Vernon Art and Science Inc. may be held responsible for any loss or damage caused or alleged to be caused directly or indirectly by the information contained in it.

Every effort has been made to trace all copyright holders, but if any have been inadvertently overlooked the publisher will be pleased to include any necessary credits in any subsequent reprint or edition.

To Fabrizio, for his continuous love and support

Table of contents

Introduction: What does it take to teach as argument? ix

    Main argument skills

    Key argument skill No1: Constructing and identifying valid arguments

    Key argument skill No2: Supporting arguments

    Key argument skill No3: Considering alternative arguments and/or counterarguments

    Key argument skill No4: Anticipating or replying to counterarguments

    Some Truths About Teaching As Argument

    What this book is about

Chapter 1   **Argumentation as part of the instructional design process**   1

    Strategies vs techniques under an ID perspective

    Argumentative discourse: What is it all about?

    Steps in implementing argumentative discourse

    Centering on contestable questions

    Sharing responsibilities

    Discussing alternatives

    Clarifying meaning

    Connecting ideas

    Labeling moves and parts of an argument

    Tracking the line of inquiry

    Evaluating facts

    Evaluating values

    Articulating reasons

    Evaluating inferences

Chapter 2	**The role of teachers in promoting argumentation**	15

Teachers' role in promoting science argumentation in the classroom: a review of the literature

Method

Findings

Promoting argumentation in the science classroom

Does students' age make a difference?

Challenges in promoting argumentation in the science classroom

Argument-promoting discourse moves by teachers and students

Defining teacher's role in promoting (scientific) argumentation

Some implications

Chapter 3	**Potentially argumentative teaching strategies**	37

Three common methods of pedagogical inquiry

Socratic Method of Inquiry

Collaborative problem solving

Debate-based deliberation

The role and place of aporia in current pedagogies

Types of pedagogical argumentation dialogue

Conclusion

Chapter 4	**How to implement argument-based teaching in different disciplinary fields**	51

Evidence in arguments: Reinterpreting the TAP

The TAPping analytical framework

The Claim-Evidence-Reasoning framework

What counts as evidence?

Types of inferences and accountability in arguments

The importance of critique or rebuttal

Concluding remarks

Chapter 5	**Evaluating students' arguments in different fields**	67
	Critical argumentation skills and their promotion	
	The present study	
	The IMPACT project	
	Participants	
	Characteristics of the Teacher Professional Development (PD) program	
	Data collection	
	Students' written responses	
	Students' interviews	
	Data analysis methods	
	The Critical Argumentation Scheme (CAS)	
	Findings	
	From 'argument-free' to 'argument-based' teaching	
	From non-critical to critical arguments	
	Students' texts	
	Students' interviews	
Chapter 6	**Some practical implications for argument-based teaching**	87
	Identifying an issue	
	Distinguishing between explanation and argument	
	Framing the activity	
	What does this mean in practice?	
	Common intention	
	Knowledge construction	
	Use of evidence	
References		*105*
Appendix		*117*
	Argument-based activity in Civic education	
	Argument-based activity in History	

Table A1. Example of classroom discourse coding using TAP elements (the excerpt was translated from the original language, i.e. Portuguese).

Table A2. Coding results of all students' texts before and after teacher training.

Introduction:
What does it take to teach as argument?

In the European Recommendation for lifelong learning (EU, 2006), one of the main skills related to key competencies is argumentation, defined as the capacity "to express one´s oral and written arguments in a convincing way appropriate to the context" (p. 4). Enhancing students´ argumentation skills implies supporting their reasoning about everyday and scientific issues in ways that such reasoning becomes more critical (van Gelder, Bissett, & Cumming, 2004), contextualized (Sadler & Fowler, 2006), evaluative (Driver, Newton, & Osborne, 2000), sense-making (Berland & Reiser, 2009), and co-constructive (Baker, 2003), just to mention some of the qualities of thinking *as* argument (Kuhn, 1992).

In "Thinking as argument", Kuhn (1992) advocates the idea that, because of the fact that most people think *with* their theories and not *about* them, a principal goal of education should be to teach students how to engage in the practice of thinking, so that reflection on their own thinking, i.e. metacognition, will be enhanced. This idea-proposal of Kuhn is further supported by the fact that argument skills' acquisition forms part of a continuum, of which the upper level, which manifests mastery of the skills, does not seem to be part of the cognitive skills naturally developed among individuals until early adolescence. Therefore, creating classroom environments that will help young people further develop their argument skills is an emerging need.

Teaching as argument, first of all, implies fostering a number of key argument skills. A brief presentation of them is necessary before I present what it takes to teach as argument.

Main argument skills

Traditionally the term "argument" has been used to refer to a valid product of argumentative reasoning consisting of at least one claim and one premise, while the term "argumentation" has been used to refer to the process by which arguments are dialogically and dialectically constructed (Schwarz & Shahar, 2017). In this book, the terms "argument" and "argumentation" skills are used alternately, based on the pedagogical assumption that argument literacy presupposes the skill of engaging in critical argumentation (Osborne, 2010; McNeill, 2011). Below some key argument (or argumentation) skills will be discussed.

Key argument skill No1: Constructing and identifying valid arguments

We cannot talk about arguing when we do not have any arguments. The very first skill of arguing competently then refers to the construction of a valid argument. An argument is "a set of claims in which one or more of them –the premises- are put forward so as to offer reasons for another claim, the conclusion" (Govier, 2014; p. 1). In most of our everyday reasoning and discourse, including classroom discourse, the arguments we form cannot be judged by the standards of formal logic, that requires for valid deductive relations between all the argument elements. Instead, we use informal logic standards, according to which the validity of an argument corresponds to its *cogency*. A cogent argument is one that "has premises that are *rationally acceptable* and that support the conclusion in a way that is *relevant* and provides *good grounds*" (Govier, 2014; p. 108) (emphasis in italics added). The way that the major premise of an argument, also called "data", supports its conclusion has also been described as "warrant" and the grounds by which the warrant stands as a good one have been described as "backing" (Toulmin, 1958). What the cogency criterion tells us, is that the first thing we should look at is at the premises alone and decide whether they are rationally acceptable or not; the second thing would be to look at the warrant and the backing of the argument. This second step will be discussed in Key argument skill No2.

Based on the above, the skill of constructing a valid argument mainly corresponds to the skill of constructing an *acceptable* argument. An argument is acceptable in two broadly defined cases: (a) when it satisfies at least one of the acceptability conditions; or (b) when it does not satisfy all of the unacceptability conditions. Given the difficulty of defining, sometimes, the acceptability of certain premises, the second criterion may be very useful at times, especially when it comes to students' arguments. Govier (2014) presents a comprehensive summary of five main conditions when arguments are considered unacceptable. These are:

- When they are easily refuted or contradicted;

- When claims or premises are known a priori to be false;

- When there is inconsistency between premises (in the cases where we have more than one premises);

- When premises are stated in language that is vague or ambiguous; and

- When the premise contains (asserts or assumes) the conclusion. This latter case is also known as "begging the question", and it entails the majority of circular arguments.

Key argument skill No2: Supporting arguments

Arguing is a dialectical process, and, as such, further supporting one's arguments to a sufficient degree for them to be persuasive is an essential aspect and skill of arguing (Walton, 1998). This "further support" is usually referred to as evidence or grounds.

In her pioneering work on "Skills of argument", (Kuhn, 1991) interviewed 160 people about what they think on several everyday topics. Two of the questions that she made aimed at eliciting further support or evidence from the participants. The first one was "How do you know that x?" and the second was "If you were trying to convince someone else that your view is right, what evidence would you give to try to show this?" Although the answers to these two questions were broadly classified as evidence, either genuine or non-genuine, I will briefly show that they correspond to two different levels of justification.

The question "How do you know that x?" is distinguished from the question "Why is it so?" (Kuhn, 2001). While the second question leads to an answer of presenting a theory or a causal explanation of a phenomenon, the first question asks for a further foundation of this theory or explanation by unquestionable facts. It is this kind of evidence-based justification that an inquiry-based teaching environment asks for.

With the second question, "What would you tell someone to convince him/her that your view is right?", the dialectical aspect of argumentation becomes more evident. To be able to argue in a skillful way, finding the first available evidence to support one's view (theory, explanation) is not enough; further backing up one's arguments according to anticipated challenges is a requirement. In this case, evidence refers to the element of "backing" that needs to be sufficient in view of critical rebuttals, expressed by physically present or imaginary addressees.

Key argument skill No3: Considering alternative arguments and/or counterarguments

For someone to be able to construct a persuasive argument, considering other points of view rather than his/her own is a necessary condition. In the absence of this skill, also known as *antilogos* (Glassner & Schwarz, 2007), several reasoning biases might appear such as the *my-side* bias (Baron, 1995), meaning one's tendency towards favoring his/her own position or the *confirmation* bias, which is the "inclination to recruit and give weight to evidence that is consistent with the hypothesis in question, rather than search for inconsistent evidence that could falsify the hypothesis" (Risen & Gilovich, 2007, p. 112).

Alternative arguments or theories are taken into consideration when the person who argues accepts that there might be some other view that is also plausible on the basis of the same or similar data or grounds. Accepting this possibility does not weaken one's position; it simply opens up the space of debate for other theories and evidence to be included in the dialogic game. In the case of interpersonal argumentation, this makes a lot of sense as listening to each other's arguments is necessary for any critical discussion to take place. For skillful argumentation in educational contexts, active listening is required, meaning that participants not only allow for other voices to be heard, but also, they co-elaborate views through constructing on each other's theories and evidence.

This co-construction on each other's views must be critical. As Atwood, Turnbull, and Carpendale (2010) humorously remark, cooperative interaction is not a 'Pollyanna' conception of social life based on the uncritical acceptance of the other's contributions. In educational dialogue contexts, challenging a peer's view may be done in several ways, some of which are: a) supporting an alternative argument or theory to the one proposed by a speaker; b) rejecting a speaker's viewpoint by attacking it directly; or c) attacking a speaker's argument by countering or challenging (through critical questions) at least one of the premises on which it is based (Macagno, Mayweg-Paus, & Kuhn, 2015). This latter element is also important from a teacher's point of view. Critical questioning has been shown to be an effective technique in promoting students' argumentation (Chin & Osborne, 2010; McNeill & Pimentel, 2010).

Key argument skill No4: Anticipating or replying to counterarguments

The reply to counterarguments is another important argument skill, as it shows the strategic implementation of argumentative discourse (further explained in Chapter 1). This reply can be done either individually, in one's own discourse (e.g. written argumentation) or socially, as part of an argumentation dialogue. In the first case, i.e. individual argumentative discourse, counterarguments are anticipated by the use of rebuttals, which serve to acknowledge the possible limitations to one's own arguments. Also it is possible that a writer exposes possible counterarguments to his/her own position, and then in the end, (s)he offers what is known as an integrated or balanced argument (Nussbaum & Schraw, 2007; Kuhn & Udell, 2007), for example an essay weighing both sides of an ill-defined issue.

As part of an argumentation dialogue, replying to counterarguments might take several forms. The strongest one is the rebuttal in the sense of a refutation of a speaker's counterargument. The function of this dialogue move, which is different than Toulmin's rebuttal explained in Chapter 1, is to "eliminate or reduce the force of a partner's counterargument by critiquing it, thereby restoring force to one's own argument" (Felton & Kuhn, 2001; p. 145). Other types of reacting to an objection exist. Leitão (2000) mentions: the dismissals, which are a kind of weak rebuttals; local agreements, which are forms of shifting the focus of the dialogue from the counterargument to one's original position through an apparent agreement with some points of the counterargument; and integrative replies, which are efforts of integrating some of the contents of the other party's counterargument into one's own position through allowing for some exceptions and conditions (this case is similar to the integrated argument in the case of individual, written argumentation).

Some Truths About Teaching As Argument

I will now briefly explain what *teaching as argument* implies, through making explicit some truths that are generally and commonly shared among researchers and practitioners in the field of argument as a teaching practice.

Truth No1: Teaching as argument is not the same as teaching how to argue.

The explicit teaching of argumentation is shown to be an essential part of helping students arriving at their mastery level of argument skills. Especially studies in scientific contexts (e.g. Bell & Linn, 2000; Zohar & Nemet, 2002) have shown the potential of the explicit argumentation instruction in favoring learners' skills and quality of arguing. Such an explicit instruction refers to "the direct teaching of various aspects of argumentation including instruction pertaining to the various definitions, structure, function, and application of arguments, and the criteria used to assess the validity of arguments" (McDonald, 2010; p. 1138). I refer to this practice as "teaching how to argue." On the other side of argument-based teaching, there exists a practice that focuses on the use, by the teachers, of strategies that allow for argument skills to be manifested in their own and students' discourse. I refer to this second practice as "teaching *as* argument."

Truth No2: For teachers to be able to teach as argument, they first need to be able to think as argument themselves

This truth comes to complement the previous one. For teachers to be able to embrace the argument constructs as part of their instruction, they must be able to apply the main argument skills themselves, such as evaluating evidence, assessing alternatives, establishing the validity of claims, and addressing counterarguments. This is why the explicit instruction of argument elements, such as the TAP elements, often forms part of teachers' training on argumentation (see, for example, Sadler, 2006).

Truth No3: In order to teach teachers how to teach as argument, a wisdom of practice must be built and shared

An enculturation into argumentation as a socio-discursive practice has thus far only focused on students. Ford (2008), for example, claimed that if students want to act like scientists, in the broader sense, they must "know how to play the roles of constructor and critiquer appropriately" (p. 416). Teachers as argument-scaffolders must not only know the same but also know how to facilitate and promote constructive argumentative dialogue and discourse in their classrooms. This requires a certain pedagogical practice knowledge that must not be kept implicit, but it should be shared, in order to be learnt and consciously applied. Defining the "wisdom of practice" necessary for argument-based teaching and unveiling the competences that teachers must have to be able to successfully promote argumentation in their classrooms is a principal challenge for teacher educators. Such wisdom does not only imply that a teacher professional is able of "practicing and understanding his or her craft", but also of "communicating the reasons for professional decisions and actions to others" (Shulman, 1987; p. 13). Therefore, creating a community of teachers able to teach as argument is a matter of communicating their acquired wisdom of practice, as a result of adequate professional training programs and initiatives.

What this book is about

This book is based on the main findings of a vast and continuous research in the field of Argumentation and Education. This means that from a theoretical point of view, it does not invent anything new. Its main contribution lies in the intersection between academic research, on one hand, and meaningful teaching practice in schools, on the other. My goal is to provide some insights to educators from any part of the world on what it means to be "argumentative" teachers in their classrooms. The existing researchers' interest has mainly focused on the argument aspects of science teaching, due to the evident relations between argumentative and scientific reasoning. This book tends to be interdisciplinary, taking into account different areas in which argumentation may be applied. Last but not least, although the teaching insights included in this book are based on my own experience as an educator of middle-grade teachers, the applicability of the principles and strategies presented transcends the age level of the students in a way to make the same knowledge accessible by every teacher, from primary school to University, interested in implementing argumentation as a teaching practice.

This book is structured as follows: Chapter 1 gives an overview of what strategic implementation of argumentative discourse in the classroom refers to; Chapter 2 is a literature review on teachers' role in promoting argumentation; Chapter 3 is a philosophical discussion on which are some potentially argumentative dialogues and how teachers may empower them; Chapter 4 focuses on the implementation of argument-based teaching in different disciplinary fields; Chapter 5 describes the impact of argument-based teaching on students' critical argumentation skills; and Chapter 6 offers some practical implications which aim to serve as summarizing guidelines for argument-based teaching implementation.

The work described in Chapter 5 is a component of an exploratory one-year project titled IMPACT (IMproving instructional Practices through Argument-based Classroom Teaching) that was supported by an internal fund for international projects granted by the author's institution. The goals of this project were: (a) to create a community of practice among teachers from different disciplines and schools in the broader area of Lisbon, Portugal, interested in implementing argumentation strategies in their classrooms; (b) to support participant teachers in the implementation of the learnt strategies through engaging them as active stakeholders in the project; and (c) to contextualize the innovative approach of argument-based teaching within methodological and empirical contributions with a wide impact, not necessarily restricted to one disciplinary area.

Although explicit reference to the IMPACT project that inspired and formed the basis of this book is only made in Chapter 5, there are short references to the Project (with the first letter intentionally capitalized) at several points throughout the book.

At this point, the author would like to express her acknowledgement to the following entities that supported this work: the Portuguese Foundation for Science and Technology (post-doctoral grant No. SFRH/BPD/109331/2015), the Faculty of Social Sciences and Humanities of the Universidade Nova de Lisboa, and the two schools that actively participated in the Project, namely: the Escola Secundária Rainha Dona Amélia, and the Escola Secundária Pedro Nunes. I am particularly grateful to all the teachers and their students who participated in the Project. I would like to especially thank the following teachers, who were actively engaged with the design of their own argument-based teaching materials and activities, part of which are included in the Appendix, namely: Filipa Baretto, Maria Paula Pereira, Leonor Santos, and Maria-José Vilas Boas.

Chapter 3 is a reproduction of a previously published article in the Journal of Philosophy of Education (license number: 4446501362338). For the original publication, refer to:

> Rapanta, C. (2018). Potentially argumentative teaching strategies – and how to empower them. *Journal of Philosophy of Education*, doi: 10.1111/1467-9752.12304

Chapter 1

Argumentation as part of the instructional design process

Regarding how and when argument skills develop better, researchers agree on that although argument ability develops with age, its mastery depends on a series of factors (Kuhn, 1992; Felton, 2004). Arguing with peers is one of these factors that have gained much attention in the literature (e.g. Kuhn, Shaw, & Felton, 1997). However, in order for classroom argumentation to be meaningful, a series of variables need to be taken into consideration such as the materials used, the type of the task and how it is organized, the goal of arguing made explicit, and last but not least, the teachers' preparedness for such activities to take place in a "full" and systematic way.

The role of teachers in implementing argumentation strategies as part of their own pedagogical kit is a fundamental aspect of argument-based teaching. According to existing literature, teachers' pedagogical content knowledge (PCK) of argumentation consists of various areas. Firstly, knowledge of students' conceptions mainly refers to the degree to which teachers are aware of their students' prior knowledge as well as their level of difficulties with specific science concepts (Avraamidou & Zembal-Saul, 2005). Prior knowledge refers both to students' current understanding of scientific phenomena and to their conceptions about the nature and structure of scientific argumentation (McNeill & Knight, 2013). Knowledge of students' conceptions is necessary for teachers being able to promote students' conceptual change, when necessary.

Secondly, for teachers to be "change agents" several instructional strategies need to be available in their knowledge repository (Sampson & Blanchard, 2012). For example, they need to address concrete student difficulties and at the same time establish commonly shared dialogic norms by everyone, so that one student's challenge becomes a classroom's learning goal (McNeill & Knight, 2013). A deep understanding of scientific argumentation and arguments themselves is necessary for teachers to be able to identify student challenges and to guide scientific argumentation as a dialogic practice in the classroom (Evagorou & Dillon, 2011). This understanding is mainly manifested in two types of knowledge: (a) knowing how to assess students' arguments (Sampson & Blanchard, 2012; McNeill et al., 2016); and (b) knowing how to reply to students' arguments, in ways that are different to the IRE (Inquiry-Response-Evaluation) pattern (Martin & Hand, 2009).

Last but not least, teachers must know how to transform their classroom into a scientific community of practice. This approach, which implies that students engage in the practices of knowledge construction, requires a view of science and science learning as being constructed through social discourse "in which artifacts (...) are questioned, evaluated and revised" (Berland & Reiser, 2009; p. 27). This would also imply that science teachers do not only develop their skills of teaching science based on argument, but also of *talking science* based on argument, as Christodoulou and Osborne (2014) remark.

Overall, teachers' PCK should address equally all the above, as they are complementary aspects of what teachers need to know in order to be able to successfully promote argumentation in their classrooms. As a result, a more holistic and integrative approach of PCK is necessary. I refer to this approach as strategic implementation of argumentative discourse. In order to explain this approach, I will take the following steps. First, I will make the distinction between strategy and technique under an instructional design (ID) point of view. Then I will explain what argumentative discourse is about. And finally, I will present the 11 steps of argumentative discourse implementation proposed by Reznitskaya and her colleagues (Reznitskaya & Wilkinson, 2017; Reznitskaya et al., 2016) as part of their dialogic teaching project.

Strategies vs techniques under an ID perspective

The distinction between techniques and strategies is not straightforward, as there is a variety in the use of these two terms for instructional purposes. Before I explain how this distinction is used throughout this book, I will first present the main definition and elements of ID.

ID refers to "the intentional and systemic action of teaching, that includes planning, developing and use of methods, techniques, activities, materials, events and educational products in specific didactic situations, with the aim of facilitating human learning on the basis of known principles of learning and instruction" (Filatro & Piconez, 2004; p. 65; translated from Portuguese by the author). In this sense, we may speak of 'instruction' instead of 'teaching' when the teaching process is directed to at least one clear objective, and both the process and the objective are more or less planned (Romiszowksi, 2016). Because of the fact that the majority of decisions from the part of the instructional designers –in this case, the professors- are intuitive (Dicks & Ives, 2008), helping them make those decisions explicit is often considered an essential part of their professional development, mainly to support the integration of argumentative elements in the existing teaching practices (Sadler, 2006; Wilkinson et al., 2017).

Figure 1.1 shows a simple representation of the ID main elements and the relations between them. The strategic elements are represented by the one-way arrows, whereas the technical elements by the two-way arrows. It can be further said that the themes, structure and objectives are the elements mostly related to strategies, whereas the materials and activities are the elements mostly related to techniques.

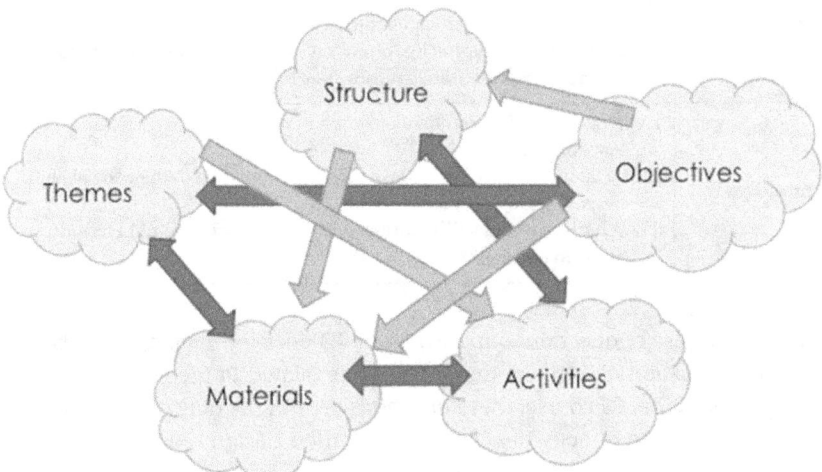

Figure 1.1. *The main ID elements.*

In general, "techniques" are the concrete ways in which teachers use the various tools, whereas "strategies" refer to the general methods or plans for which the various techniques are implemented. If argumentation is considered a pedagogical tool, it can be inferred that techniques are the concrete materials and activities that teachers design and/or use in relation to argument goals, whereas strategies describe the type of actions and methods that are applied in order to promote and facilitate the achievement of such goals.

Similarly, when teachers start implementing argumentation as part of their pedagogical practice, a series of ID decisions need to be made beforehand. For example, integrating argumentation as part of their teaching strategies implies integrating argumentative elements in (at least) each one of the main ID strategic elements, identified in Figure 1.1 as themes, structure, and objectives. An example of identifying how argumentation may form part of teachers' ID decisions is presented in Table 1.

Table 1. Integrating argumentation as part of ID decisions.

ID elements	Questions supporting ID decision-making
Themes	1. What are the principal thematic areas to treat today/during the week/ in this trimester? 2. What is the relation between them? 3. **What are some topics/issues that are offered for argumentation?**
Structure	1. How can I better structure the main contents of this subject? 2. How each main content area is structured in terms of facts, procedures, processes, principles, and concepts? 3. **How can information be "chunked" in ways that allows space for learners' argumentative reasoning?**
Objectives	1. What would I like students to learn in relation to the curriculum contents of this unit? 2. What would I like students to improve in relation to their social abilities, i.e. in class, in groups, etc.? 3. **What argument skills, both cognitive and social, would I like students to manifest?**

In the examples of questions supporting the ID decision-making of a teacher, the third question of each set (in emphasis) is related to the implementation of argumentation. Of course, these questions are not the only ones that can be asked. In the case of activities, for example, their design requires a separate view of the strategic elements included in the activities. Examples of three activities designed by teachers in their efforts to implement argumentation in their classrooms are presented in the Appendix.

The focus of this chapter and of this book as a whole is on the argumentation strategies that can be applied in the classroom, as an everyday part of the teachers' discourse. As a result, a further explanation of what is meant by argumentative discourse will hereby follow.

Argumentative discourse: What is it all about?

What is nowadays known as Toulmin's Argument Pattern (TAP) was first proposed by Toulmin (1958) in his pioneering work titled "The uses of argument". Although the book is still considered a masterpiece in Philosophy for a series of other reasons, it only became known in education because of the simple schematization on an argument and its main elements (see Figure 1.2).

Briefly, the TAP manifests the argumentative function of six elements composing the main pattern of an argument. Basically, an argument is a conclusion or a claim supported by some facts, also called "data" in Toulmin's terms. The relation between the facts (data) and the conclusion (claim) is mediated by the "warrant" and the "backing." The function of the warrant is to guarantee the logical relation between the data and the claim, whereas the function of the backing is to give grounds for both the warrant and the data to be plausible enough so that the claim is valid. When it comes to the conclusion, this is mediated by two more elements: the rebuttal, which refers to limitations or restrictions to the acceptability of the claim/conclusion, and the qualifiers (expressed by "probably") that measure the plausibility of the conclusion in a given context.

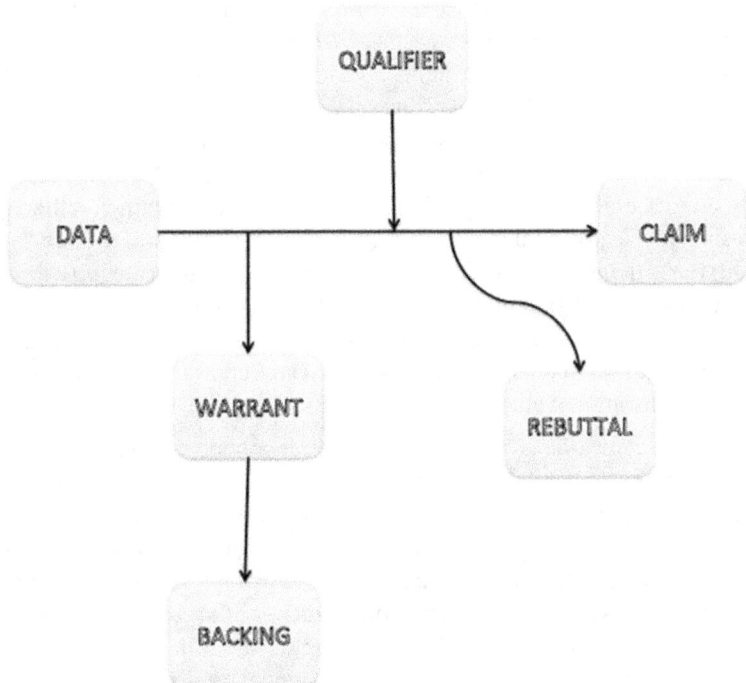

Figure 1.2. *The argument pattern according to Toulmin (1958).*

Rapanta, Garcia-Mila, & Gilabert (2013) reviewed 97 studies in order to describe how argumentative competence is conceived by educational researchers. They propose three general conceptions of argument, as form, as strategy, and as goal, and three main levels of argument assessment, namely metacognitive, metastrategic and epistemological. Among the findings, TAP is used by more than two thirds of the total studies that define argument as form, and mainly when the task is written argumentation, showing its strong connection with structural elements of argumentation. On the other hand, when the focus of the study is argument strategy or goals, TAP is hardly used. In support of this finding, Nussbaum (2011) argues that other frameworks of argumentation rather than Toulmin's may be used for both research and practice in education, such as Walton´s dialogue theory or even Bayesian models of everyday arguments. Both tools provide a detailed focus on important aspects of in-class argumentation, such as plausibility and dialecticity. Yet, their application in educational research is still stunted.

Some of the reasons for the predominance of TAP in the field of learning sciences are the following: (a) its strong connection with science and scientific reasoning (Duschl & Osborne, 2002); (b) its success in coding large data protocols (Voss, 2005); and (c) its easiness to use as a measurement of both teaching and learning performance (Erduran, Simon, & Osborne, 2004). Nonetheless, TAP has also received several criticisms, such as: (a) the model concentrates on the proponent (Leitão, 2000), (b) it can be difficult to structure reasoning in real time (Simon, Erduran, & Osborne, 2006), (c) we should study argumentation in a more holistic and emergent manner rather than imposing an existing analytical pattern such as TAP (Sampson & Clark, 2008), and (d) the scheme is restricted to short arguments and the categories impose ambiguities (Kelly, Druker, & Chen, 1998). Apart from the criticisms and the expressed difficulties when using TAP, educational researchers still consider it as a handy tool when analyzing and assessing students' arguments, especially in science education (Sampson & Clark, 2008).

However practical as a solution, it would have been quite limiting to describe argumentative discourse only based on TAP elements. In fact, in the tradition of argumentation theory, two predominant concepts or types of argument exist: the *argument1* type, which refers to the arguments as products-in-interaction rather than to the process of argumentation; and the *argument2* type, which refers to the process of arguing, i.e. something that a person engages with rather than something (s)he makes (O' Keefe, 1992). Although TAP offers itself as an adequate tool for identifying and coding arguments-as-products, other, more dialogue-appropriate schemes have been proposed to analyze the argument-as-process aspects of argumentation. For example, Felton and Kuhn (2001) and Felton (2004) propose a coding scheme for coding dialogue moves in an argumentation dialogue, consisting of 25 utterance types, including acts such as: agree, clarify, add, dismiss, interpret, etc.

Special attention needs to be given to the argumentative discourse analysis ideas contributed by the Canadian author Doug Walton. His main contributions applied in the educational field may be summarized into the following two: a) the proposal of a list of argumentation schemes, which are structures of inference that represent common types of arguments represented by a structure of a claim and at least two premises (Walton, 1996;

Walton, Reed, & Macagno, 2008); and b) the proposal of a list of argumentation dialogues, which are currently identified as seven types, namely: information-seeking, inquiry, discovery, negotiation, persuasion, deliberation, and eristic dialogue (Walton, 2008, 2011). This latter "tool" of identifying and categorizing argumentative discourse at a dialogic sequence level will be further discussed in Chapter 3.

Steps in implementing argumentative discourse

Teachers' implementation of argumentative discourse in the classroom requires the implementation of a dialogue-based pedagogy, and mostly what is known as dialogic teaching (Alexander, 2008). This type of teaching was proposed as an alternative to the *authoritative teaching*, which cannot ensure meaningful learning (Aguiar, Mortimer, & Scott, 2010). In the authoritative mode of teaching, interaction with the students is possible, but it usually takes the Initiation-Reply-Evaluation (IRE) form, in which the teacher poses a question, the student answers it, and the teacher evaluates it as 'right' or 'wrong' (Mehan, 1979). Although this pattern may be potentially dialogic, and even argumentative, as I will explain in Chapter 3, most of the times teachers initiate the IRE sequence already knowing the answer they are searching for. In that case, the dialogue looks more like a cross-examination rather than a genuine information seeking or inquiry sequence.

Recently, the Argumentation Rating Tool (ART) was developed as part of a Northamerican project on dialogic teaching (Reznitskaya & Wilkinson, 2017). The tool combines dialogic teaching steps with four main classroom argumentation goals, being that argumentation must be: 1) shared, in the sense of exploratory; 2) clear, in regards to structure and language; 3) accepted, in the sense that reasons and evidence are well-examined and accurate; and 4) logical, in the way positions, reasons, and evidence are connected. Table 2 presents a simplified version of the ART tool (for more information on the tool see Reznitskaya et al., 2016, or contact directly the main author, Dr. Alina Reznitskaya, Montclair State University, USA).

The steps above were used as the basis for a self-evaluation rubric in the IMPACT project, on which the present book was based, as explained in the Introduction. Below I offer a short explanation of each one these steps with examples of how they were implemented and perceived by the participant teachers in the IMPACT project. The examples are translated in English from the original language (Portuguese), and they represent parts of the self-evaluation reports of the teachers who participated in the Project (see also Chapter 5).

Table 2. A simplified version of the ART tool proposed by Reznitskaya and colleagues (Reznitskaya & Wilkinson, 2017; Reznitskaya et al., 2016).

Argumentation goals	Dialogic teaching steps
1. Argumentation is **SHARED**	1. Centering on contestable questions
	2. Sharing responsibilities
	3. Discussing alternatives
2. Argumentation is **CLEAR**	4. Clarifying meaning
	5. Connecting ideas
	6. Labeling moves and parts of an argument
	7. Tracking the line of inquiry
3. Argumentation is **ACCEPTED**	8. Evaluating facts
	9. Evaluating values
4. Argumentation is **LOGICAL**	10. Articulating reasons
	11. Evaluating inferences

Centering on contestable questions

The first step in implementing argumentative discourse in the classroom is about making the right questions, through transforming contents given as known into debatable issues. The Project participants achieved this in different ways, as shown in Table 3.

Table 3. Examples of ways of centering on contestable questions.

Civic Education teacher	"(…) I started perceiving the contestable affirmations and questions that were *conducting into a greater capacity of inquiry*. This was the opening phase."
Natural Sciences Teacher	"The questions must stimulate the *abductive reasoning* type, they must *create curiosity* and *stimulate the creativity*, which is something, to my surprise, I thought I was doing but I didn't…"
History Teacher	"I therefore had to choose questions that really provoked argumentation, and *not a mere explanation of a given content*. In the end, this obliged me to think of argumentative questions that promoted different types of reasoning – inductive, deductive, or abductive. It was a challenge that turned out to be really difficult and made me *think about the teacher's discursive role*."

Note: Emphasis was added in italics by the author.

Sharing responsibilities

Sharing responsibilities refers to the teacher's capacity of distributing the task of knowledge construction between herself and the students. This was made possible through different strategies implemented by the teachers, as shown in Table 4.

Table 4. Examples of ways of sharing responsibilities.

History Teacher	"(…) I had to ultimately re-think the way in which I was sharing responsibilities, searching for alternative strategies that would sufficiently *clarify roles and functions* for each part."
Natural Sciences Teacher	"I recognized that there should be created a *dialogic space among the students* and ask for the opinion of students who usually do not participate. The argumentative activities *give voice to these students*, and, for that, I started to invite them to share their knowledge with the class, calling them preferably by their names, after listening to those who always talk and like to intervene. I noted that after insisting for a while, they also started to participate, manifesting, however shyly, their opinions."

Note: Emphasis was added in italics by the author.

Discussing alternatives

The discussion of alternatives was principally manifested as an opening of the dialogue space in the classroom, and the transformation of the latter into a space where any contribution has a value because everything forms part of an inquiry. Table 5 presents some examples of how this was perceived from part of the teachers.

Table 5. Examples of how to discuss alternatives.

Civic Education Teacher	"I more often allow them to doubt and to have their own opinion; I listen to them with greater attention. I put more effort in *leaving space for their personal interpretation.*"
Science Teacher	"In the discipline of Physics and Chemistry, leading with evidence, elaborating arguments, *counter-arguing, elaborating alternative theories and refuting*, are essential activities of scientific research that do not need to be within a laboratory, it is enough to have a problem that needs to be solved."

Note: Emphasis was added in italics by the author.

Clarifying meaning

The effort of clarifying meanings was manifested in two main ways, as it can be seen in Table 6: in relation to the argumentation process itself, as well as in relation to the grounds that are used to justify students' arguments.

Table 6. Examples of clarifying meaning.

Natural Sciences Teacher	"(…) I slowly understood that in her discursive role, the teacher has to use a clear language, *the goals of argumentation must be explicit* and explained to the students since the beginning."
History Teacher	"It was relevant the fact that the students were gradually getting used to *clarify and ground their replies*, presenting data that would prove their arguments."

Note: Emphasis was added in italics by the author.

Connecting ideas

The connection of ideas was another fulfilled goal of the teachers, as it was manifested in their understanding of how they can help students to make this connection better. Some examples are presented in Table 7.

Table 7. Examples of how to connect ideas.

Natural Sciences Teacher	"(…) the ideas need to be connected and the students need to be helped in establishing the connections between their ideas/opinions and the scientific explanations."
Civic Education Teacher	"At a language level, the grammar connectors and the expressions of coordination between diverse phrases and ideas (e.g. now, but, therefore, however, as it is observed/known, etc.) get more used and with a bigger attention and care."

Labeling moves and parts of an argument

The teachers managed to identify and name the argument elements used in their discourse, either as part of the activities designed by them with the goal of arguing, or in their everyday discourse and questions as it can be seen in Table 8.

Argumentation as part of the instructional design process 11

Table 8. Examples of labeling moves and parts of an argument.

History Teacher	"At a first place, students had to, individually, express their opinion, based on evidence, about the following statement: 'During the period of Cold War, there was verified an alternate succession of phases of conflicts and quiet'. In continuation, the students had to present their arguments in their groups, learn to accept different positions and rebut the evidence of the opponents."
Civic Education Teacher	"The students' errors present numerous possibilities to argue; they are true opportunities of learning and of promoting their self-esteem. Why are you saying so? How did you arrive at this conclusion? How come? Did you forget to refer to this or that fact?"

Tracking the line of inquiry

The tracking of the line of inquiry was an important part of the argumentative discourse implementation, especially for the three History teachers. Different strategies were implemented for that, as Table 9 shows.

Table 9. Examples of tracking the line of inquiry.

History Teacher	"(…) we were guided to highlight the deep implications that this permanent process has for the teacher's discourse in the classroom, given that she has to have consciousness of the type of reasoning that she wants to encourage students to engage with: an inductive-explanatory reasoning, through previously selecting data that guide students to a certain conclusion; or an abductive-argumentative reasoning that looks for assertions that require students to give justifications, data and evidence that prove the arguments or rebuttals that they themselves expose during debate."
History Teacher	"It was made clear that it was necessary to demarcate, for the students, the line of inquiry, through documents and instructions that would orient their argumentative work. It was also important that I would guide them in articulating questions, through dialogue as a resource, and through presenting them a synthesis of the work done based on the right evidence about the issue under discussion."

Evaluating facts

The four steps that follow refer to the goal of producing logical and acceptable arguments. Although the teachers show some evidence of paying more attention at some parameters related to argument evaluation as result of their teaching-as-argument training, these two goals of 'accepted' and 'logical' argumentation remained less fulfilled, maybe because of the short training time. However, I will still present some evidence of how teachers pursued the four steps related to the above-mentioned goals, although they recognized the difficulty in achieving them. Tables 10 to 13 present some important manifestations of these goals as expressed in the teachers' self-evaluation reports for each one of the steps.

Table 10. Manifestation of the importance of evaluating facts.

History Teacher	"That class [she refers to a training session on argument evaluation] strengthened my gain of consciousness regarding the way in which I should evaluate the argumentative production of the students (…) in relation to their competence of expressing and defending ideas, both orally and in written form, constructing meanings with a historic-scientific quality. It was also important to evaluate the student's capacity of recognizing that there could exist different viewpoints about an event."
Civic Education Teacher	"Verifying what they say, the examples they give, and the factuality of their arguments forms part of the process (…) In the classroom, mainly regarding oral expression, concretizing this evaluation is sometimes difficult and requires much of my attention all discursive moments of the students. This evaluation requires a training and a good capacity of memorizing and quick interpretation of the words pronounced by the students."

Evaluating values

Table 11. Manifestation of the importance of evaluating values.

Natural Sciences Teacher	"All facts need to be evaluated, as well as the values because everything that is said is possible to be accepted and the student has to have consciousness about this."
History Teacher	"(…) as a teacher, I still have to gain consciousness regarding a permanent exercise during the argumentative debate, the one of evaluating the major or minor validity of the facts and the underlying values of the affirmations uttered by the students."

Articulating reasons

Table 12. Manifestation of the importance of articulating reasons.

History Teacher	"This made me understand that the dialogic argumentation has to lie on evidence that at the same time require a constant mobilization of data and information. This articulation between contents, so central in the teacher's work, required a choice in the activities and questions that would bring students to gradually perform that same articulation through argumentative discourse."
Natural Sciences Teacher	"(…) the reasons need to be articulated, verifying which are the levels of evidence and finally evaluate the inferences, a reasoning process through which a proposition is considered true through its connection with other propositions already known to be true."

Evaluating inferences

Table 13. Manifestation of the importance of evaluating inferences.

History Teacher	"I had to equate whether the students' replies were representing a scientific claim, informed by historical data, and which was the logical and conceptual relevance between the argumentative elements presented by them."
History Teacher	"(…) we need to know how to help students to make explicit their theories or explanatory arguments, which obliges us for a constant evaluation of the questions and inferences they come up with."

Chapter 2

The role of teachers in promoting argumentation

In general, research suggests that there are three main approaches focusing on different aspects of arguing as a classroom practice: the substantive, syntactic, and epistemological approach. The substantive approach refers to deepening students´ knowledge, in terms of the prevailing concepts, theories, and principles of the discipline (Kelly, Druker, & Chen, 1998; Herrenkohl et al., 1999). This is the "arguing to learn" approach, in which learning progression is often measured in terms of content use and level of abstraction of knowledge (von Aufschaiter et al., 2008). The syntactic approach, also known as "learning to argue", refers to the forms of evidence, methods of inquiry and analysis, and their valid application when constructing scientific and argumentative knowledge. In any argumentative situation, learners are confronted with new concepts, theories, and evidence, which they are asked to use and integrate efficiently in order to make sense of scientific phenomena (Berland & Reiser, 2009). Scientific inquiry forms part of this process, as learners need to critically search for and select information and knowledge in order to produce evidence-based arguments. Finally, the epistemological approach views scientific argumentation as an important tool allowing students to act like scientists, in the sense of implementing practices of thinking and doing science as argument (Kuhn, 2010).

In regards to teaching, "arguing to learn" focuses on the pedagogical function of argumentation and its use as a method of learning. This approach involves several questions for the teachers and the researchers in the area, such as: how students develop and improve their scientific knowledge, how this knowledge is integrated into their own discourse, and how the quantity and quality of their arguments are influenced by their content specific knowledge (von Aufschnaiter, Erduran, Osborne, & Simon, 2008). For example, in their experimental study, Zohar and Nemet (2002) not only found that the argument quality increased as a result of the explicit teaching of argument but also that the specific (biological) knowledge was used more frequently in the experimental group arguments than in the control group.

Similarly, teachers implementing the "learning to argue" approach are interested in the implementation of explicit instruction on argumentation with the aim of teaching the various definitions, structure, functions, applications, and criteria of evaluation of arguments (McDonald, 2010). The general goal is to improve learners' problem-solving skills and argumentation performance (Chinn, 2011). For this, computer tools may play an important role, as they may guide the arguing process through structuring and visualization (Lund, Molinari, Séjourné, & Baker, 2007) or they may help for breaking down complex tasks (Hmelo-Silver, 2011). The main teacher's task in the case of computer-supported collaborative learning-to-argue situations is to prompt students to use particular reasoning strategies for the tasks they are engaged with (Chinn, 2011). In other cases, teachers either prepare students for the argumentative activity (e.g. Bell & Lin, 2000) or engage with them in argumentative discussions (Reznitskaya et al., 2001).

Finally, the epistemological approach of argumentation is probably the most complex approach as it entails learners´ enculturation into science (Driver et al., 2000; Manz, 2014). In order for such enculturation to take place, students, first of all, should be given more opportunities to "talk" science rather than engage in the teacher-directed triadic talk, in which the teacher initiates a question, the students respond, and then the teacher evaluates the response – also known as the IRE pattern (Mehan, 1979; Lemke, 1990). This pedagogical shift can take place in various ways. For instance, Scott, Mortimer, and Aguiar (2006) describe how dialogic and authoritative discourse may alternate per communication episode and per role (teacher or student) leading to what is known as "productive disciplinary engagement." Similarly, Larrain, Freire, and Howe (2014) talk about three main discourse patterns that are possible to emerge in the classroom, only the third one being truly dialogic: a) Teacher-centered one-sided reasoning, i.e. teachers answering their own "why" questions as a form of involving students in their own chain of reasoning; b) one-sided co-reasoning, i.e. teachers leading students´ thinking in a hypothetic-deductive way constructing common and cumulative reasoning; and c) student-centered dialectical reasoning, in which students are empowered and take their own initiative for presenting argumentative questions and counter-opinions. For the latter to take place, a deep understanding of the norms and importance of argumentation is necessary.

Several review articles focus on the implementation of argumentation practices in the science classroom (e.g. Manz, 2014; Cavagnetto, 2010; Sadler, 2004; Sampson & Clark, 2008). For example, Cavagnetto (2010) conducted a qualitative literature review on K-12 argument interventions with three foci: nature of interventions, their emphasis, and the aspects of science included on those. He concluded with three orientations, namely: (a) immersion in science, (b) learning the structure of argument, and (c) focusing on socio-scientific issues. This latter formed the context of research for another review article, by Sadler (2004), which emphasized on the importance of the discussion of socio-scientific issues for both students' science content learning and development of argumentation skills. The review by Sampson and Clark (2008) again focuses on student´s arguments and the ways they are assessed by different analytical frameworks. In general, very few studies have focused on teacher's role in promoting science argumentation. In these cases, teachers function as the main scaffold or facilitators of various scaffolding techniques that assist students in their argumentative activities. However, our knowledge of how such facilitation takes or should take place is very limited. A thorough look at some key empirical studies is necessary for teachers and researchers to better understand the complex pedagogical phenomenon of promoting argument-based practices in the science classroom as it *actually* happens, and not as a hypothetical or prescriptive scenario. Moreover, I will focus on science argumentation, as it is the one that has received major attention from educational researchers.

Teachers' role in promoting science argumentation in the classroom: a review of the literature

Scientific reasoning, i.e. the capacity to reason like scientists, has been often compared to argumentation, i.e. the process of producing dialogically valid arguments. This is mainly based on the fact that scientists do argue in order to come up with new ideas, to better back up the existing theories, or to establish connections between theories, evidence, and counterevidence. However, classroom discourse about scientific phenomena has not much in common with what scientists do when they argue. In science, discussions focus on the inquiry of the best evidence possible to support a claim (Driver, Newton, & Osborne, 2000); in the science classroom, inquiry often stops at the first satisficing evidence which would correspond to a student´s answer considered as "correct" by the teacher (Lemke, 1990). Scientists co-ordinate theories and evidence in ways that scientific phenomena inter-relate to each other and to the existing data in multiple ways (Latour, 1987); science textbooks usually tie to one theory that best represents the opinion of the scientific community without explaining how scientists came up with this theory at a first place (Russ et al., 2009). Scientific reasoning entails confrontation and potential destruction of contradictory claims because of stronger evidence until a theory predominates over others and becomes a paradigm. But "science students accept theories on the authority of teacher and text, not because of evidence" (Thomas Kuhn, 1970; p. 80).

The need for more scientific reasoning to emerge in the classroom is strongly related to the promotion of argumentative practices by the teacher. For instance, when the teacher decides that students should *do* science rather than *learn* science, a slow but evident transformation of the classroom into a community of practice takes place. As Driver et al. (2000) observe, in science, conceptual challenge and anomalous data are per se ineffective; it is through social construction and re-construction, guided by the teachers, that students adopt scientific reasoning skills. Enculturating students as learners into modes of discourse that resemble those of a constructive scientific community is important for their deep learning of scientific practices based on their own experiences and gained knowledge (Duschl & Osborne, 2002; Manz, 2014).

Similarly, when science teachers adopt an argument-based pedagogy, significant differences in the way learners and teachers interact, talk and learn take place. Changing the class culture into one where active construction of arguments by students is appreciated rather than neglected may bring significant results to both the enhancement of reasoning skills and their gain of scientific knowledge (Zohar & Nemet, 2002; Simon et al., 2006).

Research in science education and argumentation has taken place in the last decades in order to reveal some of the best teaching practices that promote argument-based pedagogies in the classroom (e.g. Jiménez-Aleixandre, Rodriguez, & Duschl, 2000; Osborne, Erduran, & Simon, 2004; Sadler, 2006). Moreover, some researchers have opted to focus on the identification of constraints, concerns, and difficulties that science K-12 teachers face when in their attempts to implement argumentation activities (e.g. McDonald, 2010; McNeill, Pimentel, & Strauss, 2013). Nonetheless, at the time of practice, no clear guidelines exist on what, how, when, and what for science teachers should do in order to design and implement argument-based curricula. Given the importance of the matter and its central place in recent teacher professional development efforts, the present literature review endeavors to give a critical and integrative review of science teaching practice in relation to how argumentative discourse is actually being promoted in the classroom.

Method

The purpose of this review is to organize, integrate, and summarize *empirical studies* related to the actual role of teachers in promoting argumentation in the science classroom, either as part of an intervention or as part of a naturalistic design setting. The importance of teachers' role for classroom-based argumentation and teachers' preparedness for this role have been the subject of numerous contributions in the field of science education (e.g. Oman-Bekiroglu & Aydeniz, 2013; McNeill et al., 2013; Knight-Bardsley & McNeill, 2016). The present review focuses only on the studies reporting findings related to concrete actions performed by science teachers, which have been shown effective for the promotion of argumentation among students or between teachers and students.

The search of articles was done primarily using the Web of Science database, due to its variety, multidisciplinarity, and high quality of articles included. In an initial attempt, the generic keywords "argument*", "science", and "classroom" were used in the topic search area. A total of 426 articles appeared, which were screened on the unique criterion of including the keyword "argument*" also in their title. This decision resulted in 97 articles, which were subset to two types of screening: the first one was based on the abstract and gave a total of 51 articles; the second one was based on the full text and resulted in 34 articles. Both screenings were based on a series of inclusion criteria, which were the following:

C1. Does the study focus on in-service teachers or classroom practice of pre-service teachers?

C2. Does the study focus on classroom-based argumentation and its actual implementation by teachers and students?

C3. Is it an empirical study with an explicit focus on the role of teachers?

C4. Do the topics include one or more of the following: socio-scientific issues, physics, chemistry, biology, or natural sciences?

The same criteria were then applied to the references of the 34 articles, giving a final sample of 37 articles, reporting a total of 33 studies (three of the studies were reported in more than one publication). Figure 2.1 shows some main demographic characteristics of the studies included in the review, which will be described in detail in the Findings section.

Authors	Date	Country	Subject	Grade	N (teachers)	Interviews	ClassObserv	Other
Newton et al.	1999	UK	Various	7th-11th	14	✓	✓	-
Avraamidou & Zembal-Saul	2005	USA	Science	5th	1	✓	✓	-
Abi-El-Mona & Abd-El-Khalick	2006	USA	Chemistry	10th	1	✓	✓	✓
McNeill	2008	USA	Chemistry	7th	6	✓	✓	✓
Martin & Hand	2009	USA	Science	5th	1	-	✓	-
McNeill & Pimentel	2010	USA	SSI	11th & 12th	3	-	✓	-
Chin & Osborne	2010	USA	Physics*	7th-9th	3	-	✓	-
Dawson & Venville	2010	Australia	SSI	10th	1	-	✓	-
Loucas et al.	2012	Cyprus	Science	5th	1	-	✓	-
Berland & Hammer	2012	USA	Biology	6th	1	-	✓	-
Sampson & Blanchard	2012	USA	Various	6th-12th	30	✓	-	✓
McNeill & Knight	2013	USA	Science	All	45	-	-	✓
Christodoulou & Osborne	2014	UK	Science	8th-9th	1	-	✓	-
Yun & Kim	2014	Korea	Biology*	8th	1	✓	✓	✓
Larrain et al.	2014	Chile	Various	5th & 7th	153	-	✓	-
Hundal et al.	2014	USA	Envir. Health	7th-9th	2	✓	-	✓
Schoerning et al.	2015	USA	Science	3rd-5th	76	-	✓	-
Shemwell et al.	2015	USA	Science	8th	18	✓	-	✓
McNeill et al.	2016	USA	Various	7th-9th	24	✓	-	✓
Chen et al.	2016	USA	Science	1st-3rd	3	✓	✓	✓
Herrenkohl et al.	1999/2013	USA	Physics*	3rd-5th	2	-	✓	✓
Osborne et al./Simon et al.	2004/06	UK	SSI	8th	12	-	✓	-
Park	2006/08	Korea	Physics*	5th-8th	9	✓	✓	✓
Berland & Reiser	2009/11	USA	Biology*	6th & 7th	3	-	✓	-

Figure 2.1. *Demographic characteristics of the studies included in the review.*

The research questions this review attempted to reply were the following:

RQ1: How is argumentation promoted in the science classroom in relation to the instructional design decisions teachers take, especially when it comes to successful tools, techniques and strategies teachers use? Does students' age influence these decisions?

RQ2: What are some main challenges reported by teachers implementing argumentation in their classrooms?

RQ3: What are some of the main discourse moves that teachers can implement as part of their argument-based teaching in order to promote students' argumentation?

Findings

Before addressing the above questions, some general information of the reviewed studies will be presented to better contextualize the findings. Subsequently, the answers to the research questions as emerged from the meta-analysis will be reported in three separate parts, corresponding to the focus of each question.

Out of the 33 studies, 21 took place in the USA, three in the UK, and one for each one of the following countries: France, Australia, Korea, Chile, Cyprus, South Africa, Turkey, Singapore, and Taiwan. Among the subject matters taught, 11 focused on general science, four on biology, three on chemistry, three on physics, four on socio-scientific issues (SSI), one on natural sciences, and seven involved more than one science-related discipline. The number of teacher participants in each study ranged from one to 153. The teachers were from different grades giving a representative sample of K-12 education. Fifteen of the 33 studies described an argument-based classroom intervention, 10 followed a naturalistic design, whereas 8 were based on assessing teachers own perceptions of the use of argumentation in the classroom.

Several methods of data collection and analysis have been applied by the various researchers, with classroom observation and discourse being the most common (16 studies), followed by interviews (13 studies) and questionnaire-based assessment (8 studies). As far as the method of argumentation analysis is concerned, many of the reviewed studies (14) used either the Toulmin Argument Pattern (TAP) or its adaptations. Nonetheless, the majority of the studies (16) used methods of classroom discourse analysis adapted for each study's needs. These include frame analysis (Berland & Hammer, 2012; Hundal et al., 2014) and grounded discourse analysis (Avraamidou & Zembal-Saul, 2005; Yun & Kim, 2014).

Promoting argumentation in the science classroom

Based on the distinction between "strategies" and "techniques" discussed in Chapter 1, and on the important aspect of pedagogical tools that teachers use as parts of their activities to promote argumentation, the ID aspects of the reviewed studies were limited in the following three, namely: successful tools, techniques and strategies that promote students' argumentation.

Successful tools. By tools, I mean all the tangible artefacts used as part of instructional strategies, in order to stimulate, guide, or scaffold argumentation activities. Although many studies propose some tools, in the sense described above, there is a lack of homogeneity regarding the nature and function of such. However, the following categorization among types of tools was possible to be extracted, namely: (a) Maps, graphs, and charts; (b) writing templates, sheets or frames; and (c) other creative artefacts. Each one of these categories is explained below:

   a) *Maps, graphs, and charts.* Maps refer mainly to concept maps representing students' prior understanding of the topic under discussion (Chen et al., 2016). Graphs refer to graphical representations of numerical data that students may use as evidence to support their arguments (Berland & Hammer, 2012). Charts were used by Herrenkohl and Cornelius (2013) to represent students' theories and questions, and their evolution throughout the activity.

   b) *Writing templates, sheets or frames.* This was the most frequent type of tools used in the reviewed studies. Templates refer to either the Science Heuristic Writing (SHW) template (Choi et al., 2015) or to general discussion templates (Chin & Teou, 2009). Writing frames as a particular type of template were also used (Erduran et al., 2004). Finally, different types of worksheets were common among different studies. For example, teachers in Chen et al. (2016) used learning sheets containing prompts for different argument components, whereas teachers in Yun and Kim (2014) used answer sheets containing students' opinion and how they compare it with other students' opinions in their group.

   c) *Other creative artefacts.* Other creative artefacts have been used by teachers around the world in order to guide, structure, and stimulate argumentation in their classrooms. Some of them are: film clips (Lin & Mintzes, 2010), boards and posters (Herrenkohl & Cornelius, 2013), concept cartoons (Chin & Teou, 2009), and "ambiguous" objects (Varelas et al., 2008).

Successful techniques. The techniques implemented by the teachers in the reviewed studies correspond to the following groups: (a) Structuring techniques, (b) class discussion/reflection, (c) questions, (d) role assignment, (e) debate, and (f) other tool-related techniques. Here is a brief explanation for each:

a) *Structuring techniques.* This group refers to the particular ways in which teachers structure the argumentative activities in the reviewed studies. It includes techniques such as: starting an activity with a "hook" (Lin & Mintzes, 2010; Hundal et al., 2014); provide a series of steps through oral, written, or visual prompts (Bulgren et al., 2014; Chin & Osborne, 2010); or proposing a communication activity at the last lesson of each unit (Hundal et al., 2014). Structuring techniques may also refer to the way teachers structure the student groups; for instance, in Chin & Osborne (2010), teachers opt for groups of students who differ in their views.

b) *Class discussion/reflection.* Reflective discourse is another common technique among K-12 teachers in the reviewed studies. This type of discourse is commonly manifested as a generalized class discussion on a particular topic, as for example the importance of evidence and persuasion in science (Berland & Reiser, 2009) or the fact of students holding opposing points of views on the same issue (Erduran et al., 2004). In other cases, it may involve several goals such as: clarify meanings, consider multiple views, and reflect on students' own thinking and those of their classmates (McNeill & Pimentel, 2010).

c) *Questions.* Questions have a central place in promoting argumentation. They can be of several types, such as: basic inquiry questions (Martin & Hand, 2009; Chin & Osborne, 2010; Larrain et al., 2014), "hooking" questions (Lin & Mintzes, 2010; Hundal et al., 2015), or metacognitive questions (Yun & Kim, 2014), of the type "How do you know?", "What is your evidence for?", "What reasons do you have?" (Erduran et al., 2004).

d) *Role assignment.* Role-playing and/or the simple assignment of discussion roles are also commonly used among science teachers, as several studies show (Herrenkohl & Cornelius, 2013; Lin & Mintzes, 2010; Simon et al., 2006; Archilla, 2015).

e) *Debate.* Debate is another technique commonly used to support argumentation. Also, for science education goals, it has been used as an effective technique by teachers in several studies (Simon et al., 2006; Hundal et al., 2014; Lin & Mintzes, 2010).

f) *Other tool-related techniques.* Other techniques that appear less frequently because they relate to the use of specific tools appear under this category. Examples are: manipulation of "ambiguous" objects for science discussion purposes, such as the shaving cream or the baggie with air (Varelas et al., 2008); cooperative learning techniques, such as "round robin" or "roundtable" (Chin & Teou, 2009); argument evaluation techniques, such as the "cue, do and review" (Bulgren et al., 2014).

Successful strategies. By successful strategies, I mean discursive methods, which have been shown effective in terms of achieving pre-defined pedagogic objectives, related to learning and/or argumentation. The following categories emerged from the meta-analysis: (a) Focus on evidence, (b) focus on reasoning structure and relationships, (c) use of guiding questions and prompts, (d) fostering counter-argumentation, (e) emphasizing the need for consensus, and (f) other strategies. Each category is explained below:

a) *Focus on evidence.* The focus on evidence was evident in many of the reviewed studies as a teaching strategy. For example, Avraamidou and Zembal-Saul (2005) emphasize on teachers' efforts to provide students with opportunities to collect, record, and represent evidence, on the one hand, and to construct evidence-based explanations, on the other. The explicit need to support ideas with evidence was also used as a teaching strategy in Simon et al. (2006), Berland and Reiser (2009), McNeill and Pimentel (2010), Berland and Hammer (2012), Sampson and Blanchard (2012), Herrenkohl and Cornelius (2013), Gray and Kang (2014), Yun and Kim (2014), Choi et al. (2015), etc.

b) *Focus on reasoning structure and relationships.* This strategy highlights teachers' emphasis on students' understanding of the reasoning elements of an argument and the relationships between them. Teachers may help students understand the relationship between predictions, evidence and theories (Herrenkohl & Cornelius, 2013), or make connections between formal ideas and intuitively plausible ones (Hutchison & Hammer, 2010). In other cases, the focus is placed on the structure of the argument; for instance, by teaching students the components and language of argumentation (Chin & Osborne, 2010), or by making the rationale behind scientific explanations explicit (McNeill, 2009).

c) *Use of guiding questions and prompts.* As seen in Techniques, questions are an important element of promoting argumentation in the classroom. As a strategy, questioning refers to the conscious use of different types of questions for different types of activities. Some of the studies that place a particular focus on this strategy are: Choi et al. (2015), Chin and Teou (2009), Chin and Osborne (2010), Bulgren et al. (2014). A specific type of questioning includes the revoicing of a student's idea, in which the teacher restates a student's question and re-addresses it to the whole classroom (Louca, Zacharia, & Tzialli, 2012; Chin & Teou, 2009).

d) *Fostering counter-argumentation.* Supporting and fostering counter-argumentation among students emerged as another common teaching strategy, including several sub-strategies such as: contrasting the scientific explanations with alternative views (Christodoulou & Osborne, 2014), engaging students in critique and opposition (Erduran et al., 2004; Christodoulou & Osborne, 2014), or encouraging the anticipation of counterarguments (Simon et al., 2006). Playing devil's advocate was also commonly reported (Simon et al., 2006; Braund et al., 2013).

e) *Emphasizing the need for consensus.* Making explicit the need for consensus was another strategy proven effective in promoting argumentation in the science classroom, as emerged in the work of several authors (Berland & Hammer, 2012; Chin & Osborne, 2010; Archilla, 2015).

f) *Other strategies.* Other strategies include: encouraging productive framing versus correctness (Hutchison & Hammer, 2010), asking students about their mind-change (Simon et al., 2006), or making connections to students' prior knowledge (McNeill, 2009).

Does students' age make a difference?

To the question whether the tools, techniques, and strategies implemented by teachers to promote argumentation differ according to children's age, the comparative analysis showed on Tables 14, 15, and 16 implies a positive answer. Although the data are too limited to allow for a statistical comparison, the visual representation according to students' age level shows a clear tendency: the older the students become, the more explicit the need for discourse-based strategies rather than tools or techniques gets. Of the 11 studies in the 6-10 years old category, seven implement some type of tool to promote argumentation; this number becomes less for the next level age category (4 out of 10 studies), and even lesser for the oldest students (1 out of 6 studies). The contrary happens with the strategies: although all studies (6 out of 6) focusing on older students use some type of strategy, the number is reduced (8/10 and 8/11) for the middle age and youngest students. Not only the number, but also the type of strategies changes; for example, "re-voicing" is a strategy that emerges only for the 6-10 years old students, similarly to the "focus on the argument structure" that emerges as an exclusive strategy for the 11-14 year-olds. The studies focusing on older students (15-17 years old) implement a range of different strategies, not shareable with the other ages.

Table 14. Successful tools, techniques, and strategies for students aged 6-10.

Authors	Successful tools	Successful techniques	Successful strategies
Avraamidou & Zembal-Saul (2005)			Providing students with opportunities to **collect, record and represent evidence**. Providing opportunities to construct **evidence-based explanations.**
Berland & Hammer (2012)	Graphs.		Emphasizing the **need for consensus.** Emphasizing the need to support ideas with evidence.
Chen et al. (2016)	Concept maps. Worksheets.		
Choi et al. (2015)	SWH templates.	**Class discussions** to help students build their sense of what is a reasonable argument.	Scaffolding student inquiry process through **questioning**. Modeling argumentation such as informing students about scientific norms on ways how to construct claims, evidence, and relationships among data, claims, and **evidence**.

Herrenkohl & Cornelius (2013)	Theory & questions charts. Posters. SenseMaker board.	**Audience roles.**	Helping students <u>understand the relationship</u> between predictions, **evidence**, and theories.
Hutchison & Hammer (2010)			<u>Making connections</u> between formal ideas and intuitively plausible ones. **Encouraging productive framing** versus correctness (e.g. defining good wrong thinking).
Lin & Mintzes (2010)	Learning sheets. Film clips.	Structuring activities including **"hooks"**. **Questioning.** Library research. <u>Roleplay.</u> **Debate.**	
Louca et al. (2012)			<u>Re-addressing the question to the rest of the class</u>. Making clarifications. Prompting students to <u>infer relationships</u>. <u>Restating</u> students' ideas or reasoning. Giving students the responsibility of the content of the conversation. Having a large repertoire of teaching strategies from which to choose.
Martin & Hand (2009)		**"Why?" questions.**	Leading students to come up with the same question that she wanted them to study. Allowing <u>student voice</u> to affect instructional direction.
Varelas et al. (2008)	"Ambiguous" objects.	Manipulation of the objects.	
Chin & Teou (2009)	Concept cartoons. Discussion templates. Students' drawings. Paper dialogues.	Numbered heads together. Round robin. Roundtable.	Structuring cooperative learning. **Responsive questioning.** <u>Revoicing</u>, where the idea is reinforced and made available as common knowledge to all in the class.

Note: In Tables 14, 15 and 16, the formatting is intentional: underlining means that the same or similar concept appears more than once in the same column, whereas bold implies that the same or similar concept appears more than once in different age categories represented by the three tables.

Table 15. Successful tools, techniques, and strategies for students aged 11-14.

Authors	Successful tools	Successful techniques	Successful strategies
Bulgren et al. (2014)	Argumentation and Evaluation Guide (AEG)	Cue, Do, and Review.	Using guiding **questions and prompts**.
Chin & Osborne (2010)	Question Web. Conceptual resources (e.g., evidence statements or other relevant information).	Provide a structure to help students focus, organize, and verbalize their arguments both orally and visually. Organize groups with students who differ in their views. **Questions**: key inquiry, basic information, unknown/missing information, conditions, and others.	Providing scaffolds for students to ask questions (e.g., **question prompts**), make the questions explicit by writing them down, and externalize them by articulating the questions to peers. Teaching students the structural components of an argument (including the appropriate vocabulary), criteria for a good argument, and the language of argumentation. Having students work towards a consolidated and **consensual written product** that is a solution to the scientific problem that they are working on.
Christodoulou & Osborne (2014)			Contrasting the scientific explanation with other alternative views and allowing students to consider the extent to which the alternatives presented were correct, actively engaging students in the construction and critique of knowledge claims. Further questioning with providing different viewpoints or prompting students to consider other views. Providing further explanatory comments or making generalizations in the whole class.
Erduran et al. (2004)	Writing frames.	Reflective talk about opposing points of view. **Questions** such as: How do you know? What is your evidence for? What reasons do you have?	Encouraging opposition through using questions such as How would you argue against that? Or What evidence would you provide to show him that his idea is wrong?
Hundal et al. (2014)		Engagement ('hook') questions. A communication activity in the last lesson of each unit. **Debate.**	

Authors	Successful tools	Successful techniques	Successful strategies
Larrain et al. (2014)		"Why" and "What if" **questions.**	
McNeill (2009)			Making the <u>rationale and scientific explanations</u> explicit. Connecting to everyday explanations and students' prior knowledge. Providing feedback.
McNeill & Pimentel (2010)		<u>Reflective discourse:</u> when students (1) make their meanings clear, (2) consider multiple views, and (3) reflect on their thinking and those of their classmates.	Making sure that <u>argument structure</u> (claim, **evidence**, reasoning) is prevalent.
Simon et al. (2006)		**Role-playing. Debate.**	Encouraging listening and <u>reflection</u>. Encouraging and prompting justification. Defining and exemplifying argument. **Playing devil's advocate.** Encouraging evaluation using **<u>evidence</u>** and <u>anticipation of counterarguments</u>. Asking about mind-change.
Yun & Kim (2014)	Answer sheets.	<u>Metacognitive questions.</u> **The role of host** to direct discussions.	Using an invalid sample claim as an example of presenting claims based on **<u>evidence</u>** collected. **Encouraging productive framing.**

Table 16. Successful tools, techniques, and strategies for students aged 15-17.

Authors	Successful tools	Successful techniques	Successful strategies
Archila (2015)		**Role-playing.** Historical controversy.	Emphasizing the importance of achieving **consensus.** Adopting the role of facilitator and challenger.
Berland & Reiser (2009)		**Class discussion** on the importance of evidence and persuasion in science.	Encouraging students to make persuasive statements and to differentiate between their **evidence** and inferences.
Braund et al. (2013)			**Playing devil's advocate.** Focusing on inclusive argument rather than outright contradiction.

Dawson & Venville (2010)	Writing frames.		Same as Simon et al. (2006).
Gray & Kang (2014)			Supporting scientific claims by **evidence** (data and warrants) given by multiple data sources.
Sampson & Blanchard (2012)			Examining the nature of the explanations in light of the other explanations. Expand on explanations. Using data and reasoning as **evidence** to support a chosen explanation. Pointing out why the alternative explanations are unsatisfactory.

Challenges in promoting argumentation in the science classroom

Student-related challenges. A first challenge emerged from the review, as for the implementation of argumentation in the science classroom, is the low level of students´ preparedness. It is commonly reported that students´ attitudes towards science are undeveloped (Abi-El-Mona & Abd-El-Khalick, 2006; Sampson & Blanchard, 2012), and that their level of interacting with evidence is low (Berland & Reiser, 2009; Hundal, Levin, & Keselman, 2014; Lin & Mintzes, 2010; Yun & Kim, 2014). Other authors (Herrenkohl & Cornelius, 2013; Choi, Klein, & Hershberger, 2015) report the lack of students' critical thinking ability or their low conceptual and epistemological understanding as the main barriers to the implementation of argumentative practices. Finally, some authors report power issues (Yun & Kim, 2014; Schoerning et al., 2015) as the main reason for students not being able to work efficiently in groups and thus argue collaboratively with each other.

Teacher-related challenges. Part of the lack of students´ preparedness to apply argumentation in the classroom may be attributed to instructors´ lack of preparedness. The implementation of argument during science teaching requires for the creation of an authentic inquiry environment through questions and guidance (Hundal et al., 2014). For that, teachers need to be sensitive to the context and content of discourse, focus on student thinking, and apply a large repertoire of ways to respond to students´ discourse (Louca et al., 2012).

One difficulty that science teachers face, according to the reviewed studies, relates to the re-framing of classroom interaction from an authoritative or teacher-centered one to a more dialogic and student-centered interaction (Berland & Hammer, 2012). Giving students the access and power to participate in dialogue and listening to them without intervening emerges as a key issue, and challenge, for teachers' effective behavior (Erduran et al., 2004; Yun & Kim, 2014; Schoerning, et al., 2015). Another difficulty that teachers face at a personal level relates to their own confidence and use in regards to argumentative discourse and skills. This difficulty may vary from a general level, like for example limited understanding and application of argumentation (Braund, Scholtz, Sadeck, & Koopman, 2013; McNeill & Knight, 2013; Christodoulou & Osborne, 2014), to more concrete challenges, such as how to frame an argumentative question (McNeill & Knight, 2013), how to generalize (Shemwell et al. 2015), or how to align arguments with the description of scientific arguments (Sampson & Blanchard, 2012).

External challenges. By external challenges I mean all barriers that emerge in promoting argumentation in the classroom, which are not related to either the teachers or the students. As such, time and curriculum constraints emerge as the most important issue (Newton, Driver, & Osborne, 1999; Sampson & Blanchard, 2012; Hundal et al., 2014, Choi et al., 2015). Although educational policies worldwide focus more and more on the promotion of argument skills, the localized school-based norms are still constrained to teaching for assessment purposes, strictly following the prescribed curriculum.

Argument-promoting discourse moves by teachers and students

In relation to the third research question, a more thorough analysis was carried out in order to identify the concrete activities promoting argumentation in the studied classrooms. As these activities were mainly discourse-based, the focus of the analysis was the discourse moves performed by teachers only, students only, or both.

As it appears in Table 17, different types of argumentation-relevant discourse moves are proposed by the various authors (only the studies which made explicit some type of discourse moves were included in the analysis). A more careful look at the nature of the discourse moves proposed allows for the following categorization: science-related moves, critical thinking moves, and discourse facilitation moves. This categorization is in line with the three types of argument approaches discussed in the introduction as: substantive, i.e. related to the science contents, syntactic, i.e. related to the language of argumentation, and epistemological, i.e. related to the establishment of norms of argumentation in the classroom.

Table 17. Argument-promoting discourse moves by teachers and students.

Study	Teachers	Students
Abi-El-Mona & Abd-El-Khalick (2006)	Listen.	Argument from sign, example, verbal classification, expert opinion, evidence to hypothesis, analogy.
Avraamidou & Zembal-Saul (2005)	Provide students with opportunities to collect, record, and represent evidence; Provide opportunities to construct evidence-based explanations.	
Herrenkohl et al. (1999)	Establish definitions of key intellectual tools, e.g. theory; Engage the students in evaluating their own and their peers' thinking; Mirror the ideas that are in play; Shape the discourse.	Predict and theorize; Summarize results; Compare predictions and theories to results.
Herrenkohl & Cornelius (2013)	Formulate arguments; Define arguments.	Revise arguments.
Berland & Hammer (2012)		Effort to persuade each other; Assess ideas as worthy by their fit with evidence and reasoning; Controlling the topic and flow.
Berland & Reiser (2009)		Differentiate between inferences and evidence; Use of persuasive statements.
Chen et al. (2016)	Challenge/elicit; Exchange/Encourage; Lecture/Direct; Recognize/Compare/Integrate.	Retrieve; Express; Elaborate; Reframe; Defend; Synthesize; Challenge; Justify.
Chin & Osborne (2010)	Allow student-centered exploratory talk; Let students ask questions to each other; Not intervene.	Articulate puzzlement; Make explicit beliefs, claims, & (mis)conceptions; Identify key scientific concepts; Make connections between ideas & elicited explanations; Consider alternatives; Evaluate ideas critically; Challenge.
Christodoulou & Osborne (2014)	Analogy/metaphor; Argument; Compare & contrast; Counter-argument; Definitions; Description; Evaluation; Exemplification; Explanation; Generalization; Justification; Modeling; Prediction; Provide evidence; Prompts for: argument, classification, comparison, etc.	

Erduran et al. (2004).	Interpret; Justify; Ask.	Elaborate; Justify.
Larrain et al. (2014)	Elaborate follow-ups; Justifications/reasons.	Justifications/reasons; Asking for justifications/reasons; Counter-opinions.
Louca et al. (2012)	Prompt; Clarify; Evaluate student ideas or reasoning; Restate student ideas or reasoning.	Knowledge claims; Everyday experiences; Scientific reasoning & logic; Epistemologies; Direction of conversation.
Martin & Hand (2009)	Questioning that triggers divergent modes of thinking; Act as a resource person; Listen; Allow student voices to be heard; Respect students prior knowledge; Value intellectual rigor, constructive criticism, and challenging of ideas; Encourage students to generate conjectures, alternative solution strategies, and ways of interpreting evidence.	Apply elements of arguments including rebuttals; Ask questions
McNeill (2009)	Define scientific explanation; Model & critique scientific explanation; Make the rationale behind scientific explanation explicit; Connect scientific explanations to everyday explanations; Provide feedback to students; Take into account students' prior understandings or experiences; Accuracy and completeness of science content.	
McNeill et al. (2016)		Use evidence to support claims; Use scientific ideas or principles to explain the link between their evidence and claim (reasoning); Consider multiple claims.
McNeill & Pimentel (2010)	Open questions.	(Both) Claim; Evidence; Reasoning; Scientific/Personal/Other evidence.
Schoerning et al. (2015)	(Both) Use of honorifics; Discipline-specific vocabulary; Artificially low & slow speech; Fluidity of speech; Summarization; Speech between student speakers; Frequent change of speakers.	
Simon et al. (2006); Dawson & Venvville (2010)	Talk & listen; Know meaning of argument; Justify with evidence; Construct/evaluate arguments; Counter-argue/debate; Reflect on argument process.	Claim; Data; Backing; Warrant; Rebuttal.
Yun & Kim (2014)		Introduce; Respond; Add; Tune; Extend; Synthesize; Clarify; Request; Skeptical; Refute.

Science-related moves. These are the discursive moves manifesting teachers' and students' knowledge and use of scientific reasoning and explanations. When it comes to teachers, these moves include the following: providing students with feedback, resources, and opportunities to collect, record and represent evidence (Avraamidou & Zembal-Saul, 2005; McNeill, 2009; Martin & Hand, 2009); establish definitions of key intellectual tools, e.g. theory (Herrenkohl et al., 1999); modeling, predicting, and generalizing (Christodoulou & Osborne, 2014). As a result of this attitude, students become able to predict and theorize, as well as to compare predictions and theories to results. They are also able to identify key scientific concepts, make connections between elicited ideas and explanations, and manifest scientific reasoning and epistemologies based on both empirical data and everyday experiences.

Critical thinking moves. This category refers to discursive moves, which reveal teachers and students' understanding of the functions of critical thinking, as a main component of argumentation. From the teachers' part, these moves include: value intellectual rigor, constructive criticism, and challenging of ideas (Martin & Hand, 2009); make explicit beliefs, claims, and (mis)conceptions (Chin & Osborne, 2010); produce and evaluate reasons, evidence, and counter-arguments (Simon et al., 2006; McNeill & Pimentel, 2010; Chin & Osborne, 2010; Larrain et al., 2014); challenge opposing viewpoints and trigger divergent modes of thinking through open questioning (Martin & Hand, 2009; McNeill & Pimentel, 2010; Chin & Osborne, 2010); make use of the right prompts to stimulate students´ critical thinking (Louca et al., 2012; Cristodoulou & Osborne, 2014). In terms of students´ critical thinking moves, these are manifested either as argument structures and/or as argument processes.

Argument structures may refer to main argument components such as the ones proposed by Toulmin (1958), namely claim, data, backing, warrant and rebuttal (Simon et al., 2006; Martin & Hand, 2009; Dawson & Venville, 2010; Louca et al., 2012), or more sophisticated structures such as Walton´s (1996) argumentation schemes (Abi-El-Mona & Abd-El-Khalick, 2006). Regarding argument processes, focus has been placed on the differentiation between inferences and evidence (Berland & Reiser, 2009), on students´ efforts to persuade and challenge each other (Berland & Reiser, 2009; Chin & Osborne, 2010; Berland & Hammer, 2012), or on their discursive attempts to construct argumentative knowledge alone or with others through different types of epistemic and dialogical moves (Louca et al., 2012; Larrain et al., 2014; Yun & Kim, 2014; Chen, Hand, & Norton-Meier, 2016).

Discourse facilitation moves. These moves refer only to teachers and their actions related to facilitating students' discourse, and in particular, dialogue. Some of these moves are: "engaging", "encouraging", "providing", "allowing", "articulating" and "listening to" students´ discourse. Allowing students voices and questions to be heard and student-centered exploratory talk to take place without intervening is of great importance (Simon et al., 2006; Martin & Hand, 2009; Chin & Osborne, 2010; Larrain et al., 2014). Moreover, authors stress the ability of teachers to ask (Erduran et al.; Chin & Osborne, 2010; Larrain et al., 2014; Chen et al., 2016) and to articulate students´ discourse through mirroring their ideas or elaborating follow-ups (Herrenkohl et al., 1999; Chin & Osborne, 2010; Larrain et al., 2014).

Defining teacher's role in promoting (scientific) argumentation

Based on the findings, teachers´ argument-promoting discourse activities may be classified into, at least, three types, according to the role adapted each time by the participants. The first type refers to the role of *teacher as dialogue facilitator,* the second to *teacher as critical thinker,* and the third to *teacher as a scientist.*

Teacher as dialogue facilitator. In order to facilitate dialogue, teachers, first of all, must make sure that they allow for dialogic discussion to take place, through listening to what students have to say and through prompting interaction and co-construction among students. Although listening is self-defined, prompting and encouraging dialogue is not always easy. Here are some ways of doing that according to our findings:

- Formulating questions in ways that allow multiple answers to emerge and inviting students to do the same. Examples of such questions are: How do you know? What is your evidence for? What reasons do you have? etc.

- Making sure that there is a concrete goal to be reached at the end of the activity, for example, a group of students having different viewpoints on an issue arriving at one common solution; and

- Explaining and giving importance to the concrete functions of argumentation. Some of these functions are the following: the construction of an argument composed by at least one claim and a reason, the justification of the claim based on evidence, the consideration of alternative points of view on the same issue, the evaluation of reasons and types of evidence to arrive at the most plausible theory, and the need to respond adequately to counterarguments and rebuttals.

Teacher as critical thinker. Critical thinking and argumentation are two terms often encountered together in educational research studies, many times being used alternately or one serving the other. In this book, the author adopts the view that critical thinking refers to some general skills such as empathy and critical detachment (Walton, 1989), which are straightforwardly developed through engagement in argumentative dialogue. As Walton puts it:

"In teaching critical thinking successfully, both teacher and students bring with them developed skills, at various levels, of interpreting and evaluating extended sequences of argument discourse in natural language. Each field or discipline has its own special knowledge and vocabulary. But the common core of basic critical thinking skills underlying critical reasoning in each discipline is the key ability to look at both sides of an argument. The structure behind this ability is the concept of argument as dialogue" (Walton, 1989: 182).

In science education, engaging students in argumentative practices may have different impacts on both students and teachers critical thinking skills. Their manifestation in discourse takes place through easily identifiable argument components, such as TAP elements or argumentation schemes. Otherwise, it is disguised in discourse moves that are considered as promoting argumentative discourse, in specific contexts. There is not one concrete dialogue analytical scheme on which the majority of educational researchers agree as the most adequate to identify classroom argumentation episodes as they emerge in natural discourse. Nonetheless, according to the review findings, the use of questions either to prompt, from the teacher´s side, or to challenge, from the students´ side, is a very common technique.

Teacher as a scientist. As scientists, teachers must be able to identify key scientific concepts, such as theory and explanation, make the rationale behind scientific explanation explicit, expand on explanations, and help students establish connections between ideas and explanations. Teachers as scientists must also be prepared to model and critique scientific explanations, connect them to everyday explanations, and check for the accuracy of scientific content. This finding is coherent with other authors' claim that scientific knowledge should form part of teachers' pedagogical content knowledge, as it affects their views of notion of science and its functions (McDonald, 2010), as well as their capacity in implementing argumentation (McNeill et al., 2013; Knight-Bardsley & McNeill, 2016), due to the resemblance between scientific and argumentative reasoning.

Some implications

Based on the reported findings, teachers all over the world face a series of challenges at the time of implementing argumentation. Some of them relate to the students, others relate to the teachers themselves, and few relate to external factors.

Student-related challenges mainly regard their limited understanding of argumentation norms and their lack of previous experience with argumentation tasks. If teachers perceive these difficulties as barriers, then it is very possible that any attempt to promote argumentation stops with a very first manifestation of students not being able to apply what the teachers ask for. As an alternative, teachers should insist on promoting students' argumentation skills, as a great part of research agrees that only after practicing them in the classroom, do students reach their maximum level of manifestation (Erduran, Simon, & Osborne, 2004; Osborne et al., 2004; McNeill & Krajcik, 2008).

Many of the reviewed empirical studies show that it is the teachers, not the students, who lack the necessary argumentation language and knowledge to apply it (e.g. Newton et al., 1999; Sampson & Blanchard, 2012; McNeill & Knight, 2013). More argument-specific pedagogical knowledge is necessary for teachers to be and feel prepared for argumentation, as also confirmed by other studies (McNeill & Knight, 2013; McNeill, González-Howard, Katsh-Singer, & Loper, 2016). Finally, although teachers often refer to the barrier of strict timings and curricula, the fact that a number of argument-based interventions have taken place thus far and in different countries is per se optimistic. A more systematic implementation and analysis of argumentation and its benefits for both teachers and students may act positively for policy makers and school directors to allow more space and time for such initiatives to occur.

Overall, teachers´ role in promoting science argumentation in the classroom emerges as crucial in all of the studies reviewed. However, argument promotion is perceived, teachers are the ones who provide both the building basis and blocks for argumentation to take place and develop during a class. Moreover, depending on how much prepared or trained they are, teachers choose from different activities and scaffolds to make sure that argumentative discourse, either oral or written, is constructed towards the right direction, which will lead to the expected outcomes. Although few scholars have stressed the importance of instructional design skills at the time of proposing argument-based activities in the classroom (e.g. Duschl & Osborne, 2002; Osborne et al., 2004; Berland & McNeill, 2010) the issue of knowing *how, for what*, and *when* argumentation should emerge is fundamental.

According to the findings of this review, the role of K-12 teachers in promoting argumentation in their classrooms is reflected in three complementary sub-roles: a) teachers should be *facilitators* of the argumentation taking place among the students; b) teachers should hold solid *scientific knowledge* of both concepts and reasoning skills; and c) teachers should be able to *think critically* by themselves and understand their students' efforts to do so, even when their manifested argument skills are still weak.

Chapter 3

Potentially argumentative teaching strategies

The intersection between critical thinking, dialogue, and inquiry has been an object of long discussions and theorizations in education all over the world. In practice, its implementation as a pedagogical paradigm has been mainly performed either at a macro-level of a curriculum innovative program, such as the well-known Philosophy for Children, or at a micro-level of educators implementing methods of pedagogical inquiry in their individual classrooms (e.g. Ellsworth, 1989; Wang, 2005). It is interesting to note that the famous Critical Pedagogy movement initially proposed by Freire and further developed by other philosophers of education such as Ira Shor, Peter McLaren, and Henry Giroux, has not yet been linked to concrete educational programs capable of applying all the big ideas that the movement represents. What we do have, however, is a vast number of educators who prove themselves as critical pedagogues, because of the strategies that they apply in their classrooms. It is this micro-level of implementation that the present article focuses on.

In this Chapter, I make explicit the role of argumentation in three of the most common inquiry-based pedagogical methods, namely the Socratic method of inquiry, collaborative problem-solving, and debate-based deliberation. Then I present some gaps in the current approaches of implementing these and other pedagogical methods, inspired by the lack of *aporetic* element in the current educational discourse about critical thinking, as Papastephanou and Angeli (2007) point out. Finally, I present an adaptation of four types of argumentation dialogues, initially proposed by Walton (2008, 2011), as providing a structured way of identifying, analysing, and guiding the implementation of "effective" pedagogical inquiries in any classroom.

The goal of this essay, previously published in the Journal of Philosophy of Education, is to define *aporia* as a manifested dialogic element. My approach of aporia rises from the definition of the *aporetic aspect of critical thinking* (Papastephanou & Angeli, 2007), as one that "considers the thematisation of established criteria of ends as the utmost manifestation of critical mentality" (p. 617). To do that, I focus on the use of dialogue, including the Socratic inquiry, as a pedagogical method that promotes collaborative inquiry between the teacher and the students, in ways that enable classroom-based interaction to reach an increased symmetry or contingency among unequal participants (van Lier, 1994). Although the three commonly used methods of pedagogical inquiry, presented below, create *aporia* as a reflective state, its thematisation is not pursued as a common end, thus reducing symmetry and, possibly, effectiveness. The proposal of argumentation as a systematic method of producing and pursuing *aporia* at different levels of inquiry is the main contribution of this essay.

Three common methods of pedagogical inquiry

Socratic Method of Inquiry

The Socratic method of inquiry, when applied for educational purposes, requires that teachers prepare and ask questions adapted for three phases of discussion, namely: exploration or discovery, careful examination of ideas, and extending the discussion outward.

A question that teachers should ask themselves before starting a Socratic method of inquiry is: Are there correct and incorrect answers regarding the specific issue x? If the answer is "yes", the teachers may opt for close-ended questions, which are useful if they want to place students' attention on a particular set of textual facts and initiate discussion about them. These questions, even though they are close-ended, shouldn't simply ask students to recite factual, learned information. Some examples are: "Why does X appear in that text/photo/film?", "What can we say with confidence about X?", "What role does X play in the story/photo?", etc. Each student's response may add to the collective understanding being developed by the discussion. Close-ended questions are important to establish what the group already knows about the topic before the class moves on to an open-ended discussion.

If the questions asked by the teacher do not necessarily ask for one correct answer and several answers-perspectives may be appropriate, open-ended questions are preferable. In that second type of exploration question, "negotiation of truth is possible because the question not the teacher regulates the conversation" (Schmit, 2002; p. 75). Examples of such questions are: "What does X symbolize?", "How would you interpret X?", "Which one do you think it would be a most expected action/outcome of X under conditions Y?", etc. The goal of asking an open question is to nurture shared responsibility by opening up the limits of exploration to many different interpretations of the same fact. The main hint for the successful implementation of this initial part of the Socratic method of inquiry is to establish a democratic climate where students may speak directly one to another. It is also recommendable to combine both types of questions as the defining limits of each one of them are not always clear: a question previously conceived as close-ended may turn out to be open to several answers.

The second part of the Socratic method of inquiry corresponds to what educators and educational researchers currently call a careful examination of ideas (based on the Socratic *elenchos*). The goal of this type of questioning is to model students reasoning and to ask students to examine their thinking. Type of questions used in this type of discourse are:

1) Questions of clarification

    a. What do you mean by that?

    b. Say a bit more.

    c. Can you give us an example?

2) Questions that probe assumption

    a. Why would someone say that?

    b. What do you think happened?

3) Questions that probe reasons and evidence

    a. What are your reasons for saying that?

    b. Are you saying ...?

    c. Which means ...?

4) Questions about viewpoints or perspectives

    a. What would be another way of saying that?

    b. How do X's ideas differ from Y's?

Other types of questions include: questions that probe implications and consequences, questions about the question, etc. (Yang, Newby, & Bill, 2005; Harrison & Howard, 2009).

The last part of the Socratic method of inquiry refers to teachers' efforts to extend the discussion outward. This is mainly done through generalization, i.e. through supporting students' efforts to construct or criticize generalized claims (Shemwell et al., 2015). A generalizable claim is a claim transferrable to other similar situations, based on an observation. The value of this cognitive action lies in the fact that generalization of a claim requires further justification and evidence, which in turn requires more sophisticated reasoning. Particularly for science, generalization has an additional value, as without it, students could easily come away from the activity with the mistaken idea that scientific claims should be restricted to statements of what was observed and nothing more (Shemwell et al., 2015).

Collaborative problem solving

Another commonly used method for promoting critical inquiry in the classroom is the collaborative problem solving method and techniques. According to Roschelle and Teasley (1995), "collaboration is a coordinated, synchronous activity that is the result of a continued attempt to construct and maintain a shared conception" (p. 70). When it comes to collaborative problem-solving situations, the focus of educators and researchers should be at least two-fold: on the so-called co-construction process, and on the epistemic object(s) being jointly constructed among students, and between the students and the teacher (Brough, 2012).

The idea of learning as a collective enterprise draws on the work of Dewey and is also very much related to the dialogic pedagogy paradigm promoted by Alexander (Hopkins, 2014). For Alexander (2008), pedagogy is not just a matter of teaching techniques, but it refers to "the act of teaching together with the ideas, values and collective histories which inform, shape and explain that act" (p. 92). Under this view, dialogic teaching assigns a cumulative quality to classroom talk (Mercer, Dawes, & Staarman, 2009), which may be manifested in several ways: as questions serving as building blocks for further dialogue (Alexander, 2008); as opening up the dialogue space in order for it to be co-constructed by teachers and students (Wegerif, 2008); or as leading to a type of talk initially defined by Mercer as *exploratory talk*. In all these cases teachers adopt a collaborative authority role, arranging conditions that are "conducive to community activity" (Dewey, cited in Hopkins, 2014, p. 419).

Although current implementations of collaborative problem solving methods take into account the above, no concrete "rules" exist regarding how and when teachers shall intervene in order to guarantee that constructive learning is taking place. Scholars from the computer-supported collaborative learning field claim that the mere elicitation and explicitisation of contributions are not enough for knowledge acquisition; consensus building should also be an important part of the learning task (Weinberger & Fischer, 2006). Therefore, the teachers' role should focus on structuring a task that requires consensus and applies a set of conditions that enforce collaboration between students

(Kreijns, Kirschner, & Jochems, 2003). In face-to-face classroom environments, as well, the need for consensus building has emerged as a positive factor for dialogue quality and learning in several studies (e.g. Chin & Osborne, 2010; Felton, Garcia-Mila, Villarroel, & Gilabert, 2015) applying the so-called collaborative argumentation, in which students co-construct new ideas that "integrate valid points from multiple perspectives" in order "to develop more reasoned, refined, and robust conclusions" (Felton et al., 2015; p. 373).

Debate-based deliberation

Debate, in the sense of a critical discussion, forms part of a research process, in which different proposals can be tested through systematic intersubjective verbal communication (Barth & Krabbe, 1982). What debate allows for is the development of argument literacy in its whole, as students participate in academic-style conversations, so they become better citizens and better students at the same time (Graff, 2003). As Wineburg claims, cited in Osborne (2005), "expertise in academic disciplines is not just a result of the accumulation of factual knowledge. Rather it is the result of having developed patterns of thinking appropriate to the discipline that lead the expert to see patterns, ask questions, and anticipate possibilities" (p. 41). Transferring to the K-12 classroom, helping students become academically competent implies helping them develop an advanced type of thinking, which many scholars have referred to as deliberative reasoning.

According to Berland and Reiser (2011), efficient deliberative reasoning in the classroom should serve at least two goals, namely sensemaking and persuasion, which have at least two prerequisites, use of prior knowledge and the creation of a need for debate. For the latter, Berland and Reiser (2011) argue that it is facilitated by providing the students with a complex data set that supports multiple claims, and through making explicit the epistemic goal of "consensus building which can only be accomplished when students attend and respond to one another's competing claims and evidence" (p. 199). The final aim of this type of reasoning is to decide which is the best explanation among those offered, which is at the heart of so-called *abductive* reasoning (Walton, 2005).

The role and place of aporia in current pedagogies

According to Socrates, the goal of any inquiry is the resolution of *aporia*, which for Plato was "a state of mental confusion, bewilderment, or helplessness" (Matthews, 1999; 29-30). The cause of this confusion, according to Aristotle (Topics, 6.145^{b}16-20) is "the equality of opposite reasonings", what constitutes a dialectical or two-sided issue when both explanations of a problem or a state of affairs may apply. Socrates applies *aporia* in a different but complementary sense to Aristotle. For Socrates, *aporia* is or must be created between two states and the resolution of *aporia* corresponds to the passage from the one state to the other: he "wants, *in some way*, to move from a person's claiming particular knowledge to the need of this person's claiming more general knowledge" (Politis, 2015; p. 142, emphasis in the original). The difference that is important here is not to compare the ancient philosophers' views, as this is not the goal of this article, but to use the conceptual diversity expressed in the works of Plato, Aristotle, and Socrates regarding the term *aporia* as a criterion for the different manifestations of argumentative reasoning in the three types of pedagogical dialogues previously described. This section is dedicated to identifying the *aporetic* element in the current pedagogical inquiry methods, to conclude that what current educational discourse lacks is a definition of *aporiai* as a starting point of the subsequent dialogue, which takes the form of argumentation.

In the Socratic method of inquiry, questions have a central place. These questions do not necessarily need to come from the teachers; actually it is the students' questions that better form *aporiai*, as they manifest the gap between the two cognitive states described by Socrates, the particular knowledge, on one hand, as declared in books, teachers' words, etc., and the generalized knowledge, on the other, which needs to be interiorized and applied by the students in their academic and personal lives. It is not by chance that in modern Greek *aporia* is the main word used for students' questions manifesting lack of understanding of a particular issue. As it regards teachers' questions, these do not always form *aporiai*. Most of the time, teachers' questions aim to test for knowledge in the format of posing questions rather than to create a democratic environment for knowledge construction and sharing. There is a substantial difference between asking students about their prior knowledge and asking them about their ideas; as there is a difference between asking them about what they already know, or are supposed to know, and asking them to think about how to transfer what they know to other settings.

The Socratic method of inquiry is clearly an aporia-inducing activity; however, it is not clear whether this *aporia* functions only cathartically, i.e. as a purgation of the pretence of knowledge, but also productively, i.e. as the first stirring of creative thought (Politis, 2006). In the first sense, *aporia* "is not part of the positive search for knowledge, but at most a preparation for it" (p. 86). In current educational dialogue terms, when teachers ask students about their current knowledge, the degree of *aporia* they might lead them to is mainly defined by how closed or open these questions are. The more open the question, the more difficult it becomes as the student knows that his/her answer will not be judged as either wrong or correct but as more or less relevant to what the teacher expects or defines as relevant; thus, perplexity is increased but the need to satisfy the teacher remains. Only when the teacher adopts a productive *aporia* stance, may he/she welcome all sorts of different ideas, answers, but also productive questions from part of the students. When this happens a close-ended question might also turn out to have a number of possible answers.

In order for this openness to possibilities to take place, teachers must abandon their Inquiry-Response-Evaluation (IRE) pattern (Lemke, 1990) and adopt a more student-centered approach, in which the natural emergence of dialogue between students is as welcome as one might expect. The teacher's role then is not to induce students to *aporiai* but to lead them to create such *aporiai* by themselves, and then to constructively work together in order to resolve them or to create new ones. This corresponds to a more extended view of the productive type of Socratic *aporia*, one in which the space between one state of knowledge, usually "belonging" to the teacher, and another, usually "belonging" to the students, is mediated by a commonly constructed dialogical space. Such a space might either correspond to the exploration of a particular problem (Roschelle & Teasley, 1995) or to a general meaning construction process about any issue as in a community of philosophical inquiry (Kennedy & Kennedy, 2011).

Finally, when the focus of *aporetic* discussion is concentrated on a particular issue or problem and its resolution, the Aristotelian concept of *aporia* applies. For Aristotle, the definition of the issue itself appears as more important than the solution. Once the dialectical issue has been defined, according to criteria, then it is open to exploration. This exploration might take several forms, such as exploring the issue itself (i.e. whether it is worth discussion or not), exploring interpretations of the issue (i.e. whether it is *a* or *b*), exploring problems emerging from the issue (i.e. what will happen if *a* or *b*), and lastly exploring solutions that address the issue-related problems (i.e. whether solution *a* is better than solution *b*). In all these cases an aporetic element is present. Even in the last case of finding a solution, the problem of showing which solution offers the best explanation exists. Teachers' tasks are to encourage and facilitate students' epistemic negotiation of the available solutions and to help them through an abductive reasoning process in order to decide on the most plausible arguments supporting the various solutions.

We now come to understand that what was previously described as three separate types of inquiry-based methods actually interconnect with each other; the passage from one type of dialogue method to the other largely depends on the transformation of *aporia* from a state of perplexity to a state of knowledge, and from a search for a particular answer to the search for the best explanation. However, what we haven't mentioned yet and is important for any implementation of *aporia* in the educational praxis is Plato's *aporetic* element of "reflecting on what an *aporia* is and what kind of response it calls for" (Politis, 2006; p. 100). From a teacher education point of view, this means that the most important elements in applying inquiry-based methods in the classroom is to know which methods to use and when to use them. This strategic aspect of implementing constructive pedagogical dialogue is involved in argumentation as demonstrated in the next section.

Types of pedagogical argumentation dialogue

Duschl and Osborne (2002) stand for a vision of argumentation as a dialogic discourse that furthers inquiry and not as a process that ends inquiry. Based on this view, and on the Platonic *aporetic* element of perplexity in its productive sense described above, pedagogical inquiry should be a continuum of different types of dialogues with different, each time more refined, scopes and goals. The definition of each type of argumentation dialogue and the passage from one type to another, also described as dialectical shift (Walton & Krabbe, 1995), are then essential for a systematic identification and promotion of argumentation-based inquiry in the classroom.

Douglas Walton, perhaps the contemporary philosopher who has written the most about argumentation and dialogue, proposed a total of six dialogue types (i.e. information-seeking, negotiation, deliberation, persuasion, inquiry and eristic dialogue) in his early works, to which a seventh type, i.e. discovery dialogue, was added later (Walton, 2008, 2011). Each dialogue type is defined by: an initial situation, a main goal, the participants' aims, and possible side benefits of the fulfillment of the goal. Table 18 presents an adaptation of the characteristics of four types of dialogue for the pedagogical context.

Table 18. Adaptation of Walton's types of dialogues for the pedagogical context.

Type	Initial Situation	Main Goal	Participants' Aims	Side Benefits
Information-seeking - IS	Need for shared knowledge	Make background knowledge explicit	Check knowledge Share information Build common ground	Examine previous understanding Investigate difficulties/lack of knowledge
Discovery - DS	Need for possible explanations of a problem	Find the best hypotheses for testing or analysis	Define problems Choose criteria for testing Search for evidence	Stimulate creativity Establish an environment for problem solving Stimulate curiosity

Inquiry - IN	Need for examining evidence	Find the strongest evidence	Assess evidence Interpret evidence Compare evidence Coordinate evidence with claims	Better understanding of evidence Critical standing towards sources of evidence Acquiring technical terminology
Persuasion Dialogue - PE	Alternative explanations	Find the best explanation	Persuade others Support explanations with the strongest evidence available	Develop and reveal positions Build up confidence Make a decision

The four dialogues presented in Table 18 do not exactly correspond to the three inquiry-based pedagogical methods previously presented. However, the *aporetic* element that was implicitly present in those methods is now clearly manifested in the initial situation of each type of argumentation dialogue. When the goal of the dialogue is information-seeking, the *aporia* concentrates on the search of information; when the goal is discovery, it is the search for a problem; when the goal is inquiry, it is the search of evidence to solve the problem; finally, when the goal is persuasion, the *aporia* is manifested in the search for the most adequate solution.

To illustrate how these types of dialogue emerge in a classroom, I will use two examples: the first comes from my current research with middle-grade teachers of different subject areas in Portugal; the second is an excerpt of a discussion in a 5th grade class in the US, cited in Reznitskaya and Wilkinson (2015). In the following transcript, a Portuguese 9th grade history teacher, marks a passage, with the help of her students, from inquiry to information-seeking and then to discovery dialogue (the transcript was translated from Portuguese by the author). The questions, either by the teacher or the students, which initiate each type of dialogue are printed in bold.

Teacher	So, if there are no social classes, as we already saw, as well there is no difference of (.) wealth. **And if there is no difference in wealth, what happens to people's heritage? The factories, the lands?**	IN
Many	[They go] to the state, to everyone.	
Teacher	They will belong to? (.) to the community, won't they? Therefore, they will form part of the (.)	
Many	Community.	

Teacher	Community. Now, my dear fellows, if this revolution will implement this way of thinking, one of the first measures that it will take, will be exactly to do what? (.) Come on, think.
Andre	Take the money from the people.
Teacher	What will they do? One of the first measures? (.) If they don't need social classes, they don't need to have (.)
Manel	Difference.
Teacher	Difference (.) of work, of wealth, of property, etc. etc. But did that exist in Russia? Did those differences exist or not? (.) To whom did the lands belong (.) in their majority? The big *latifundia*? The big properties?
Carla	To the noblemen.
Teacher	In their majority to the noblemen (.) and also the big industries, the big banks belonged to whom? (.) To the aristocrats, to put it simply (.) My dear (refers to a student), if the goal of the socialist revolution is to try to reach a society without classes, what would be one of the first measures for them to take?
Eva	Maybe withdraw the lands…
Carla	… the properties
Eva	The properties.
Teacher	Exactly. But explain to me how this will take place.
Eva	Withdraw the properties, if everyone is the same, there won't…there won't be some better than others.
Teacher	This comes after. The first measure, because the State still exists, the first measure that the State will take will be what? (.) Withdraw the lands from the (.) landowners (.). We call this land nationalization, and we can also use the expression "collectivization", but I like nationalization better, nationalize the property. The first, one of the first edicts that emerge later in November, as we will see, is the edict of the land (she writes on board).
Manel	**But, professor, would you like to give us a synonym of "edict"?** IS
Teacher	An edict is a document that … in which you can find laws that regulate and determine what a group of people has to do, is that clear? An edict, a land edict (.) Yeah? It is a decree, a document where laws are declared, is it clear?
Eva	(she was going to say something but stopped)
Teacher	My dear ones, come on let's think, this situation will provoke a (.)
Carla	Revolution
Teacher	And who is going to revolve now?
Many	The noblemen.

Teacher	Who has the property, obviously they will not just stay quiet to watch the land distribution, so what will happen? We will see the formation of an army who will oppose the Bolsheviks (.) now obviously this decree together with others that were coming up will create dissatisfaction primarily to the population who is touched, the big landowners. This dissatisfaction will have as a result that many of these men will form an army and ask for assistance to the countries that were defending demo-liberal regimes. This will initiate a war, a civil war (turns on the PowerPoint presentation). Here you have the three principal commissaries of the revolution, initially the most important, who were Lenin, who is the strategist of the whole revolution, then you have Trotsky, who play a very important role, not only in thinking terms, but also because he is an army general and will guide the troupes of the Red Army, which is the army that will defend the revolution.	
Andre	**Miss, is this from the communist side?**	IS
Teacher	From the socialist side, Bolsheviks, yes. After that Trotsky when the civil war starts will organize the defense of the revolution and will lead the Red Army (…) From Spring 1918 onwards, we are having the civil war between the White Army and the Red Army; the White Army is composed of the defenders of demo-liberalism and of the czar, whereas the Red Army, led by Trotsky, will defend the socialist revolution.	
Andre	Miss, was the White Army the one defended by the czar that was demo-liberal?	
Teacher	Yes (.) Now, this period, which is the period of civil war, will also be called the period of war communism (.) And it is at that time that a series of measures will be taken, such as the nationalization of the banks, the nationalization of all the industries that have more than 5 workers. During this period that is called war communism or civil war, which will take place between 1918 and 1920 (.) but already in 1918 … (She writes the date on the board).	
Rui	**Miss, what will happen in 1921?**	DS
Teacher	What happens in 1921? We are getting there. The war finishes, which is important on its own. The civil war ended. Now, during that period of war communism, more nationalizations took place (.) of banks, therefore of what sector? (.) Financial (.) Of industries, mainly of industries with strategic economic importance (.) Of transports. (She writes on board). At the same time, Russia will go through an extremely difficult phase (.) seriously difficult.	
Filipa	Miss, is this after they divided the goods?	
Teacher	Ah, but who told you that they had divided the goods? Filipa deduced it by herself, well done. It is clear that this raises a question in your minds, it should raise, but then what was the question, let's conclude the question (…)	

In the example above, the first type of dialogue initiated by the teacher is an Inquiry dialogue (IN), which aims at interpreting available evidence in order to examine the reasons behind the edict of land signed during the Soviet revolution. At several points during this part of the dialogue, the teacher invites her students to consider different types of information in order to come up with the most adequate explanation, i.e. the one that best explains the phenomenon under investigation (note that the search is about information that explains a phenomenon, not about the theory that best explains a problem, which is the case of persuasion dialogue). Moreover, the goal of the dialogue is not to share background information, but to interpret already shared knowledge in the context of inquiry of a new answer: why the edict of the land was signed. A shift to an Information-seeking (IS) dialogue is marked when Manel asks the teacher for a synonym of the word "edict". After she replies with an explanation of that, she attempts to initiate another inquiry dialogue ("*come on let's think, this situation will provoke a ...*"), which turns out to be a monologue, until another student, Andre, asks for a couple of clarifications in relation to the information previously given by the teacher in a mono-directional way. It is only after Rui's question ("*Miss, what will happen in 1921?*") that the classroom dialogue slightly changes to a discovery type: instead of asking for clarification on the given information, he goes a step further, anticipating that the situation after the civil war might be problematic. Filipa's question that follows shares the same spirit of curiosity: she anticipates a fact, the division of goods, to better contextualize the problem implicitly stated by her classmate. This short instance of a preliminary type of Discovery dialogue (DS) is interesting, as it is motivated by the students, but at the same time is limited, as it does not arrive at the main goal of a discovery dialogue, which is to find the best hypotheses for testing in regards to an ill-defined issue or problem.

The next excerpt presents a persuasion dialogue of a classroom discussion aimed at finding an answer to the question of who is responsible for the injury of a child named Zack according to evidence found in a text. The dialogue sequence starts with a teacher's open-ended question that invites students to freely talk about whom they think was responsible. The persuasive quality of the interventions is also marked by the fact that both teacher and students use argumentation language, i.e. words such as: I agree/disagree ... because, clarify, challenge, etc. It is important to note here that the teacher in the example that follows has previously received training on dialogic teaching methods, whereas the first teacher had not at the time of the interaction.

Teacher	**So, who would like to start us off this morning?** Okay, Jerry.	PE
Jerry	Well, I think the one responsible for Zack's injury would be the coach, because he was the one who let Zack play when he shouldn't because he knew that he already had an injury	

Andrew	I disagree with Jerry because it actually said in the passage that Zack thought that his team needed help, so he decided to go in, 'cause the coach wasn't trained to find a concussion. So, he decided to go in on his own, without the coach telling him to. 'Cause the coach wasn't trained to see a concussion.
Lily	I agree with Andrew because … you wouldn't let … If you know we got hurt and we insisted to go back into something like that, you would at least make sure that we're okay. And I think Zack's coach probably did that … I think Zack's coach probably made sure that he was okay, so it's not all of his fault. He as an adult should say 'No, maybe you could go back in next time'. But it's not only his fault.
Teacher	So wait, how is that agreeing with Andrew? 'Cause Andrew says it's not the coach's fault, but you're …
Lily	Yeah, I don't think it's the coach's fault either.
Teacher	But you said, 'As an adult he should know'. I'm just … I want you to just clarify.
Lily	Well okay, I agree with Andrew, like everything that he said, but it's not complete… Okay, I just agree with Andrew, like what he said. … The coach didn't say 'Zack, get back in here'. Zack wanted to and he went in on his own.
Kate	I disagree with Jerry. I don't find that it's the coach's fault because in the paragraph it says they, the coaches weren't trained at that time to know what brain concussion looks like. 'Cause brain concussions are invisible injuries, it says it in this story, so, I don't find that it's the coach's fault and …
Jerry	But Zack was hurt …
Kate	Yeah, but he said he was all right, so how is the coach supposed to know?
Teacher	OK, so let's let him respond to that. They challenged you, right? So now let's let Jerry respond … We had a few challenges, so let's let Jerry maybe respond to that challenge, and maybe, I don't know …
Jerry	But if you see someone fall down very hard on their head and come back to the bench, saying that they're alright, the coach should know that they've been in an injury, and the coach should not let them play.

In the dialogue excerpt above, which I identified as Persuasive dialogue (PE), the different explanations provided by the students are contained within a co-constructive epistemic negotiation guided by the teacher whose intervention is limited and focused on the dialogue goal. Although the implicit goal is for students to persuade each other to prefer their own explanations, the explicit goal as manifested in teacher's discourse is not to reach a final state of agreement, which would resolve the main *aporia* of who is responsible for Zack's injury, but to maintain the *aporetic* element throughout the dialogue. The concept of dialogue implemented here is very similar to the Platonic type of conversation that focuses on the "critical examination of some view, by exploring the conditions under which it would be true, and under which it would be false", as Leigh

(2007, p. 318) puts it. It is this type of critical dialogue that explores all the possibilities of pedagogical inquiry-based discourse.

Conclusion

In this Chapter, I presented argumentation dialogue as the heart of dialogue-based pedagogies. The main justification is that through a systematic conception of the different types of argumentation dialogue, such as the one presented by Walton (2008, 2011), a clearer perception and achievement of the Platonic *aporetic* element, which is the basis of critical thinking (Papastephanou & Angeli, 2007), is achieved. At the same time the Socratic idea of the passage from one epistemic state to another as a way to "resolve" *aporia*, or better said to transform it, is also clear in the variety of dialogues proposed from information-seeking to discovery to inquiry and to persuasion. Systematizing educational dialogue, in this sense, is not about prescribing it but rather *designing* it in ways that can render it more effective from a conversational point of view (Smith, 2014).

For this new, *aporia*-based pedagogy to be achieved, the use of abductive reasoning as a preferred teaching method, compared to deductive and inductive types, is necessary. According to Walton (2005), "when abductive reasoning is used, the dialogue must be regarded as open to new evidence and future developments as the dialogue proceeds" (p. 234). This idea resembles the Aristotelian dialectical process (in Greek *dialegesthai*) in which the aim of an argument is "to remove one party's doubts about some thesis or statement that is unsettled or doubtful" (ibid, p. 100). This reduction of doubt is settled through a dynamic shift of the burden of proof between the parties, and not necessarily through providing one correct solution, answer to a problem, or interpretation, which is what teachers usually do (in the same way that therapists should not provide a cure; Smith, 2014).

Applying argumentation as a method to pursue and maintain *aporia* through shifting among states of perplexity is, therefore, a challenge for educators. The issue of power and epistemic authority is an important part of this challenge, related to the virtue of having "an educated sense of one's own ignorance" as Hogan and Smith (2003; p. 170) observe. And they continue: "Such virtues are to be made explicit (…) through a reflection on what befalls experience during practices of teaching and learning" (ibid). Providing teachers with the necessary methodological tools that would help them gain consciousness of different types of dialogues and their implications for students discourse and learning is an ongoing goal for philosophers of education.

Chapter 4

How to implement argument-based teaching in different disciplinary fields

If argument-based teaching is about enculturating students into the norms and habits of reasoning of a particular scientific community, then the first question a teacher must ask is: What is the main reasoning challenge in my domain area? A mathematics teacher could answer "solving problems"; a history teacher could answer "making causal claims about historical facts"; a chemistry teacher's answer could be "reconstructing chemical reactions"; and a physics' teacher could similarly say "explaining physical phenomena". We can easily understand that the four reasoning challenges have a different quality, and thus, a different approach must be applied when teaching by argument in different disciplinary areas, as the ones mentioned.

In Mathematics, for example, the main challenge is to solve known mathematical problems. Therefore, the main triggering question will be "How can problem x be solved?". Unless problem x is a complex mathematical puzzle, for which solutions are still unknown, the focus of a mathematician is not as much on the solution, but on the discovery of a problem. In other words, a complete statement of a problem sometimes is half of the solution. Quoting Einstein: "If I had an hour to solve a problem, I'd spend 55 minutes thinking about the problem and 5 minutes thinking about solutions". Given this major challenge in the domain of Mathematics, a teacher may initiate students' reasoning by asking them to formulate problems, before asking them for ways to solve them.

An example of this is given by Lampert (1986) and her telling stories technique for teaching multiplication. She would first ask students the question "Can anyone give me a story that could go with this multiplication...12x4?" (ibid, p. 322). Her subsequent question would be "And if I did this multiplication and found the answer, what would I know about those jars and butterflies" (ibid). Only after this initial meaning giving to a mathematical operation, would the teacher move on to proposing solutions "as a joint endeavor by teacher and students, drawing on actions that make intuitive sense to the students" (ibid), as the dialogue excerpt in Table 19 shows.

Table 19. Example of mathematical problem formulation and search for solutions (from Lampert, 1986; pp. 322-324).

Teacher	Okay, here are the jars. The stars in them will stand for butterflies. Now, it will be easier for us to count how many butterflies there are altogether, if we think of the jars in groups. And as usual, the mathematician's favorite number for thinking about groups is? [Draws a loop around 10 jars]
Sally	10
Teacher	Each of these 10 jars has 4 butterflies in it, so how many butterflies are inside this circle?
John	40
Teacher	How'd you figure that out?
John	It's 4 x 10
Teacher	I put the jars in groups of 10 because I knew it would be easy for you. How many more butterflies are there outside the circle?
Jim	8
Teacher	I add 10 jars and 2 jars and I get 12 jars. Each jar has 4 butterflies in it. So how many butterflies are there altogether?
Chorus	48
Teacher	Suppose I erase my circle and go back to looking at the 12 jars again altogether. Is there any other way I could group them to make it easier for us to count all the butterflies?
Jean	You could do 6 and 6.
Teacher	Now, how many do I have in this group?
Steve	24
Teacher	How did you figure that out?
Steve	8 and 8 and 8. [He put the 6 jars together into 3 pairs, intuitively finding a grouping that made the figuring easier for him.]
Teacher	That's 3 x 8. It's also 6 x 4. Now, how many are in this group?
Jean	24. It's the same. They both have 6 jars.
Teacher	And now how many are there altogether?
Patty	24 and 24 is 48.
Teacher	Do we get the same number of butterflies as before? Why?
Patty	Yeah, because we have the same number of jars and they still have 4 butterflies in each.

In the Mathematics example above, the focus on discovering a problem before proposing ways to solve it is clear. The same can be applied in a totally different area, such as History. The main challenge of a historian is to understand why certain facts take place so that similar facts can be predicted. Therefore, searching for the "real" causes of the historical events rather than simple coincidences or unproven information is the main task. Transferred to a classroom, this may mean that a triggering question would be "How do we know that information X is true or not?" or "How do we know that event X took place because of Y?" or even "What are the facts that best explain why a certain event took place?" Deciding what counts as evidence for a particular claim among the available data is a major reasoning challenge in History.

In Science, the decision for the best explanation about why a particular phenomenon takes place is the main reasoning challenge. This challenge, in order to make sense, requires authentic scientific tasks, for which it is yet not known why theory X best explains phenomenon Y. This is very important when it comes to science education when all the science contents that students should learn are established contents, in the sense of scientific theories or explanations that have become generally accepted as the best according to criteria. When one of these theories is used to explain a phenomenon is always in relation to another theory that may explain the same phenomenon in a less complete, accurate or relevant way. This reasoning from the best explanation, which corresponds to *authentic* scientific reasoning, is also known as abductive reasoning (Walton, 2005).

The commonplace idea that Mathematics is about deductive, History about inductive, and Science about abductive reasoning is not entirely correct, although it has some part of the truth. All types of reasoning may include different types of inferences, such as the three mentioned above. As I will show further in this chapter, the decision on which type of reasoning is predominant for each disciplinary area is mainly based on the inference step producing the main claim or conclusion of an argument. Nonetheless, the relations between *all* the different argument elements and how these get established is what defines the type of reasoning used in discourse, and subsequently in teaching.

Evidence in arguments: Reinterpreting the TAP

The TAPping analytical framework

Erduran et al. (2004) propose an adaptation of TAP "as a tool for tracing the quantity and quality of argumentation in science discourse" (p. 916). Their adaptation regards two different methodological tools: (a) a quantitative one, based on the combination of two, three, or four argument components in one argumentation unit; and (b) a qualitative one, based on the identification of five levels of argumentation according to the quality of reasoning and counter-reasoning. In both cases, the unit of analysis is a sequence of classroom interaction (argumentation episodes) either with the whole class or in small groups. The five levels of argumentation quality proposed by Erduran et al. (2004) are presented in Table 20.

Table 20. The five-level qualitative scheme proposed by Erduran et al. (2004).

Level 1	Arguments that are a simple claim versus a counter-claim or a claim versus a claim.
Level 2	Arguments consisting of a claim versus a claim with either data, warrants or backings but do not contain any rebuttals.
Level 3	Arguments with a series of claims or counter-claims with either data, warrants or backings with an occasional weak rebuttal.
Level 4	Arguments with a claim with a clearly identifiable rebuttal. Such an argument may have several claims and counter-claims.
Level 5	Extended argument with more than one rebuttal.

Although the five-level coding framework has been influential among educational researchers, there are several reasons that render it difficult to apply in a variety of contexts. First of all, data, warrants and backing are considered as belonging to the same level of reasoning. This is quite problematic and incongruent with Toulmin's (1958) initial conception and description of the model. Second, the attention on rebuttals without an explicit account of how rebuttals are used in oral discourse and their relation to the existing or anticipated counter-arguments remains incomplete. Third, the topics of discussion are only of socio-scientific nature and of a low epistemic complexity (e.g. the construction of a zoo), which reduces the importance of field-dependency of the enacted argument elements.

The Claim-Evidence-Reasoning framework

McNeill et al. (2006) propose a different adaptation of TAP aimed at increasing its accessibility and its alignment with the NRC's (1996) *National Education Science Standards*. Their "instructional model of scientific explanation" (p. 158) consists of three elements, namely claim, evidence, and reasoning. According to the authors, evidence corresponds to Toulmin's data, whereas reasoning entails both warrant and backing. They further define that evidence is "*scientific* data that supports the claim" whereas reasoning is a "*justification* that shows why the data count as evidence to support the claim" (p. 158, emphasis added).

Regarding the field-dependency issue, McNeill et al. (2006) acknowledge the importance of domain-specific knowledge: "Considering the content and context is necessary for determining the appropriateness and the strength of the explanation, not just the structure alone" (p. 159). However, they also acknowledge that their model is a "generic framework across different science content areas and contexts" (p. 159). No comment is available in regards to other fields, different than science. Moreover, it is important to note that McNeill et al.'s (2006) model was not proposed as a framework to assess arguments, like in the case of Erduran et al. (2004), but as part of a scaffolding design to support and enhance students' ability to construct scientific explanations. However, the authors do offer both a generic rubric for assessing students' scientific explanations and an example of its adaptation for a specific question task, as parts of the Appendix of their 2006 paper.

According to McNeill et al.'s (2006) rubric, there are three levels (0, 1, and 2) for each one of the argument components (claim, evidence, and reasoning). Without the authors giving more details about their decision on criteria for the three levels, it is easy to identify three criteria emerging in their rubric, namely accuracy, sufficiency, and completeness. The use of these criteria, and thus the decision on which of the three levels a student's argument belongs to, is made explicit in the adaptation of the rubric for a chemistry question example (p. 190). We see there that the adaptation of the criteria is restricted to a specific example at a time, making it thus difficult for other researchers to understand the nature of the criteria used in terms of argument quality as part of a reasoning process. Although disciplinary content is taken into consideration, disciplinary reasoning, i.e. the potential differences in the types of reasoning required for arguing in different disciplinary areas, is not addressed.

What counts as evidence?

According to Informal Logicians, the field-dependency nature of Toulmin's model is problematic (Johnson, 1996; Freeman, 2006). Moreover, Freeman (2006) claims that it is not the TAP elements but "the standards for argument evaluation (that) are field dependent" (p. 103). I would add that these standards are different for each one of the considered field-dependent elements, especially the three that were considered as "evidence" and "reasoning" in McNeill et al.'s (2006) framework. These are the data, the warrants, and the backings.

The data, or grounds, correspond to "whatever detailed assemblage of facts, observations, statistical data, previous conclusions, or other specific information" a person relies on "as the immediate support for his specific claim" (Toulmin, Rieke, & Janik, 1984; p. 38). Toulmin et al. (1984) add that not all of the grounds offered by a person may equally be accepted as "data" by another person. In everyday communication, this means that a person's grounds should be "backed up" to a sufficient degree so that they obtain or increase their credibility. In science contexts, this may mean that grounds should since the beginning have some scientific weight. Otherwise they are easily rebutted and the scientific claims they are supposed to support are also rebutted. In the later case only, mainly applicable to exact sciences, do grounds/data need to correspond to some sort of evidence. Nonetheless, the type of evidence used at this first-level of reasoning is primary, in the sense that it is *the first evidence available* to make a scientific explanation sound.

In regards to warrants, I agree with the account given by Freeman (2006) that whenever warrants are made explicit, they take the form "Given data such as D, one may take it that claims such as C" (p. 101). This further implies that warrant is a generalizable rule of inference according to criteria. An example of everyday reasoning can be the following:

1) It's 30 º C (data), so a walk would be good (claim).

Example 1 is a common argument in everyday discourse, in which only a claim supported by some data is made explicit. Re-constructing the implicit premises of this enthymematic argument, i.e. an argument that lacks some of its premises, we come up with the following additional argument elements:

2) Warrant: 30º C is considered a good temperature for being outdoors.

3) Backing: The higher the temperature, the more desired a walk is.

4) Rebuttal: Unless a person feels too hot, so she would possibly prefer the swimming pool.

From the example above, it is evident that what might be a general truth for person A (i.e. *30º C is considered a good temperature for being outdoors*) might not be considered the same by person B (an implied counterclaim may be that "*30º C is too hot for being outdoors for a person coming from the Italian Alps*"). In this sense, the warrants need to be relevant for the particular context in which the claim is put forward. When warrant carries this relevance element within it, through explicitly referring to some relevant contextual elements, then it may be considered that it counts as personal evidence for the claim-data argument. An example of a contextually relevant warrant (Warrant$_R$) adapted for the case above is the following:

5) Warrant$_R$: 30º C is considered a good temperature for being outdoors *in Dubai during the month of August.*

In this sense, the warrant still has an explanatory function (like the data/grounds), but it may be considered as evidence based on personal account or experience. It is the answer to the "Why is it so?" question as Kuhn (2001) proposed. However, this simple explanatory function for everyday arguments may not be as "innocent" when it comes to science arguments. The distinction between factual evidence and personal theories or explanations is then becoming an issue, as Kuhn (2001) further argues.

Among the three TAP elements considered here, namely data, warrant, and backing, it is the backing that has a clearly justificatory function. Thus, it is where the evidence for reasoning should be looked for. The question is then: what does the backing justify? The answer adopted in this book is that backings have two potential objections of justification: both data and warrants[1]. It depends on where the burden of proof is placed in a particular context of reasoning. In oral, inter-personal argumentation this is easy to identify, as it is the interlocutor who contextualizes the "How do you know" question according to his/her "need" to be persuaded. In the temperature example mentioned above, backing may be asked for either in relation to the warrant, i.e. *How do you know that in Dubai during the month of August this temperature is good for a walk?*, or to the data itself, i.e. *How do you know that it is 30º C?*. From a quick comparison, someone can already say that the second is less possible as we take for granted that an observation of a physical phenomenon (in this case, the measurement of temperature) is held appropriately. However, that may not be the case if the same conversation was held in a laboratory, and more particularly in a science class about temperature measurements. Context is also influential when it comes to written argumentation; nonetheless, in that case, it is reduced to two main factors: (a) the type of reasoning and the internal relations established between the reasoning elements; and (b) the anticipation of an imaginary addressee's challenges and counterarguments. These two factors will also define where the evidence held by the backing will be situated and how its quality may be assessed.

---

[1] Although Toulmin (1958) only refers to backings as related to warrants, he accepts that an imaginary challenger of an argument may not only challenge the acceptability of the warrant, but also of the whole argument.

Types of inferences and accountability in arguments

In a definition attributed to the philosopher Charles Peirce, cited in (Psillos 2011), "reasoning is a process in which the reasoner is conscious that a judgment, the conclusion, is determined by other judgment or judgments, the premises, according to a general habit of thought" (pp. 121-122). In general, there are two ways in which a process of reasoning can confer justification on a belief: the first is by making the case that if the premises are true, the conclusion has to be true; the second is by rendering a belief plausible and thus making it available for further testing (Psillos, 2011). According to Peirce (1878), only that second way, which is called abduction or abductive reasoning, may produce new knowledge, and thus may be related to scientific reasoning.

The difference between deduction, induction and abduction is well illustrated in the example given by Preyer and Mans cited in Walton (2001), as presented in Table 21.

Table 21. Distinction between deductive, inductive and abductive reasoning.

Deductive	Inductive	Abductive
Suppose a bag contains only red marbles, and you take one out. You may infer that the marble is red.	Suppose you do not know the color of the marbles in the bag, and you take one out and it is red. You may infer that all the marbles in the bag are red.	Suppose you find a red marble in the vicinity of a bag of red marbles. You may infer that the marble is from the bag.

For Walton (2001), abduction is different than deduction and induction because the conclusion is just a hypothesis, a best guess, based on the given knowledge and evidence at that moment. For this reason, abductive inferences are defeasible, meaning that they are "subject to retraction if further investigation of the facts in the case shows that another of the alternative explanations is 'better'" (p. 145). Moreover, abductive reasoning resembles a continuous deliberation process that needs to be open to revision as new evidence of the factual circumstances of the case enters into the calculations. Abductive reasoning is similar to the reasoning of a detective looking for the best data that would give the best explanation possible. The decision for what counts as the best explanation in a given context is based on the criterion of plausibility, rather than possibility, as in deductive inferences, or probability, as in most inductive ones (Walton, 2001).

All arguments are inferences, and as such there must be some deductive relation between the premises and the conclusion. However, this deductive relation also known as *modus ponens* is not necessarily located between the data and the claim. This is only one case, for example in mathematical syllogisms where the relation between data and claim is quite self-proving (e.g. two plus two make four). It is also possible that the modus ponens is located between the warrant and the data, as in the case of warrant-using inductive argument. Examples are facts' interpretations in history according to a certain source, or the calculation of a statistical result applying a certain formula. Finally, there is also the possibility that the modus ponens is situated between the backing and the warrant. This refers to when certain evidence leads to the creation of certain logical syllogisms, as in the case of detectives' investigations. In that case, certainly the warrant is not pre-established, but the argument can be either inductive or abductive, being the latter case more difficult to prove.

In summary, arguments may include three types of inferences, namely *modus ponens*, inductive, or abductive (Macagno et al., 2015). In the first type, nothing may be placed under discussion (example: two plus two equals four). In the second type, the interpretation of data may be placed under discussion (example: the same temperature may be felt differently according to the place). In the third type, the argument itself may be placed under discussion (example: the need for argument-teaching that the present book proposes). The strategy for achieving stronger arguments in the second and third case is by providing relevant warrants and backings, in the sense of grounds or *evidence* that everyone involved may forcelessly accept. Their acceptance depends on how accountable both the claims and the grounds are held by the speaker or writer.

According to Ford (2008), accountability strongly relates to scientific sense making and learning. One of the ways this relation is expressed is strongly epistemic, and it might be further inferred that it applies to any kind of disciplinary knowledge, not only related to science. As Ford states, "sense making becomes scientific sense making when authority is exercised with the *knowing that* and *knowing how* involved in holding knowledge accountable" (p. 417, emphasis in the original). It is the knowledge of the methods and values applied that are relevant to an epistemic field and their more or less valid application to that field that render a piece of knowledge *accountable* in that particular field. In TAP, methods and underlying values are mainly expressed in the form of warrants when it comes to Science, but they may also be expressed in the form of backings when it comes to other disciplinary fields, such as History. To understand this distinction, I will first show the difference in what counts as a scientific claim versus what counts as a historical claim.

In Science, claims are statements that express an aspect of a manifestation of a phenomenon. Examples of scientific claims are: "Objects fall", "Atoms are separated", "Volcanos errupt". In History, claims are statements that express a value of a historical event. This value might relate either to how true (accurate, complete) the statement is, or to how an event may be assessed (importance, positive/negative, etc.). Examples of historical claims are: "World War I led to Europe's financial damage", or "The British government possesses the legitimate authority to tax the American colonies[2]". From the examples of claims above, it can be easily understood that the inquiry process is different when arguing about a claim in Science and in History. In Science, inquiry is mostly oriented towards finding and testing the hypothesis that best matches a claim, whereas in History, inquiry is oriented towards finding and evaluating the corresponding interpretation. Searching for hypotheses and searching for interpretations mark two different types (and levels) of evidence. In Science, what counts as evidence is whatever confirms or falsifies a hypothesis, whereas in History, what counts as evidence is the set of sources that give authority to the interpretation entailed in one's argument.

In TAP terms, a scientific claim will ask for scientific data to form together a model or explanation of a phenomenon. The warrant will then authorize this explanation by adding the necessary theoretical background for it to be considered as a theory. Backing will then be evidence from scientific experiments that prove this theory. Data and backing need to be different from each other; otherwise, there is pseudo-evidence instead of evidence (Kuhn, 1991). Scientific reasoning has two levels: that of making sense of a phenomenon through coordinating data, claims, and warrants (laws or theories relevant to the model created); and that of founding the theory by providing some further support that authorizes the data. It is at the second level that argumentation, in the sense of persuasion, takes place.

In History, argumentative reasoning also has two main levels, although they are slightly different than the ones described above. Level 1 corresponds to a formulation of a historical interpretation, based on primary source data, whereas level 2 corresponds to a further validation or contextualization of the interpreted facts based on secondary sources. The use of warrant is less evident in historical reasoning and it is mostly implicit like in everyday reasoning. This is because most of the time the warrants used are already established, thus taken for granted that they are shared. However, the challenge for a history teacher is to make explicit that warrants need to be made explicit, as different interpretations may apply for the same data. Warrants, in this case, might refer to the validity of the source, to the perspective adopted by the author, or to already known distinctions of same source/facts interpretations. However, what counts as evidence for a historical claim is mainly found in the backing, e.g., the justification why source A must be considered a better source than B given that argument X is based on data provided by source A.

---

[2] This example was taken from Bransford, Brown & Cocking (2000).

How to implement argument-based teaching 61

In summary, we saw that what counts as evidence may be different in different disciplinary fields. I gave the example of Science and History to support my view. In Science, evidence is mainly provided by the warrant, meaning the specific method or law applied in a proposed theory. In other words, defining whether or not a claim holds as *accountable* for a scientific community, the first thing one must see is whether or not it respects certain laws or principles. In History, evidence is mainly provided by a backing, i.e. a fact that gives force to the fact that source A is a valid historical source which someone must trust to make a historical argument X. In other words, defining whether or not a claim holds as *accountable* for a historians' community, the first thing one must see is the reliability of the sources used. Table 22 shows an example of two arguments, one from Science and another from History, and showcases what counts as data, warrant, and backing for each one of the two.

Table 22. Example of two arguments, in Science and in History, highlighting the difference of what counts as claim, data, and backing in the two disciplines.

	Science	**History**
claim	It is possible to make ice cream that doesn't melt.	Neanderthals were much more sophisticated than is popularly believed.
data	By adding a protein present in Japanese fermented soybeans called "natto".	Paintings found in three Spanish caves are over 64.000 years old.
warrant	This protein was found to fix together fat, water, and air in the ice cream.	That's 20.000 years before the first humans arrived in Europe.
backing	Experiments by Scottish scientists showed that by adding this protein, ice cream is maintained solid for a longer time.	The team behind this study used the uranium-thorium method to date tiny carbonate deposits that have built up on top of the cave paintings.

Note: The examples presented here were based on information found in the Daily Mail and National Geographic correspondingly.

The importance of critique or rebuttal

As in Science discussions in general, critique has a central place in evaluating and creating knowledge. The same applies in classroom argumentation. Before explaining how all this may be manifested in a classroom-based argumentation dialogue, in the last section of this chapter, I will now show what critique means for different disciplinary areas, its relation with the burden of proof, and its manifestation as a rebuttal in an individual argument.

In both types of reasoning seen above, i.e. the scientific and the historical, what increases the relevance and sufficiency of accounted knowledge, either in the form of warrants or backings, is the acceptability of the rebuttals against real or anticipated critiques. A critique is usually manifested in the form of counter-claims. These counter-claims focus on the weak parts of the argument and have as a goal to show that alternative interpretations may exist regarding at least one of the parts of the argument expressed by a speaker (or a writer). Critique is very important for learning through argumentation, as it leads to a better understanding of the particular type of reasoning held as *accountable* for a particular community. For example, in Science, students will learn that different theories may apply to explain the same phenomenon, and in History, different interpretations of historical data may lead to different claims.

In the previous section, I claimed that the basis of evidence for scientific reasoning lies in the warrant, whereas for historical reasoning it lies in the backing. In this section, I will show that the burden of proof in scientific reasoning mainly lies in the backing, whereas in History it mainly lies in the warrant. In simple terms, this means that a possible critique against the scientific argument presented in Table 22 will first focus on the backing, and mainly on the meaning of "maintained solid for a longer time". Does this mean that ice cream doesn't melt? What about temperature changes? Have scientists considered other variables when setting up their experiments? Instead, when looking at the historical argument, critique is more attracted by the warrant, and especially the information that "proves" that the distinction between humans and Neanderthals according to when they appeared in Earth is valid.

A possible distinction between these two types of argument and the difference in the allocation of the burden of proof, if we imagine the dialogical (scientific community, field) context in which they are expressed (Gordon, Prakken, & Walton, 2007), may lie in the type of reasoning predominant in each disciplinary field. In Science, where the goal is to create new knowledge regarding how certain phenomena work, most of the arguments used are "warrant-establishing." This means that the warrants used as part of the argument are part-and-parcel of the backings (evidence) found to support the theories that establish the specific warrants (and not others). The main function of scientific reasoning is then to identify the evidence that best matches a theory so that the warrants behind the theory hold accountable in the particular field of reasoning. This is easily understood when the warrants used for a particular scientific theory in Physics, for example, belong to another theoretical field (e.g. Mathematics). The function of the warrant may be each time different according to the argument made. Bing and Redish (2009) illustrate this very well when they talk about four types of functions mathematical warrants may take when used in Physical arguments: as a calculation; as a physical mapping; as invoking authority; and as math consistency.

In History, where the goal is to create a better understanding regarding known phenomena, also known as interpretation, most of the arguments are expected to be "warrant-using". This means that historians need to be based on a certain given interpretation, to be able to interpret something else. In other words, the new interpretation will be based on that older one. This resembles the inductive reasoning example presented in Table 21. Based on some given evidence, a claim is made. On the contrary, in scientific abductive reasoning, something is considered to be evidence as part of a theory that needs to be tested.

Taking into consideration the different types of arguments, according to the type of reasoning that lies behind them, I will now represent three different TAP versions according to whether the argument is deductive (modus ponens), inductive, or abductive. I will also indicate where the possible rebuttal may be situated, illustrated as a critical question posed by an imaginary addressee.

The first example if from Geometry and it is a deductive argument. The burden of proof in this type of argument lies in the data. This means that if we imagine that an addressee challenges the argument, it is the relation between claim and data that (s)he will challenge, as shown in Figure 4.1.

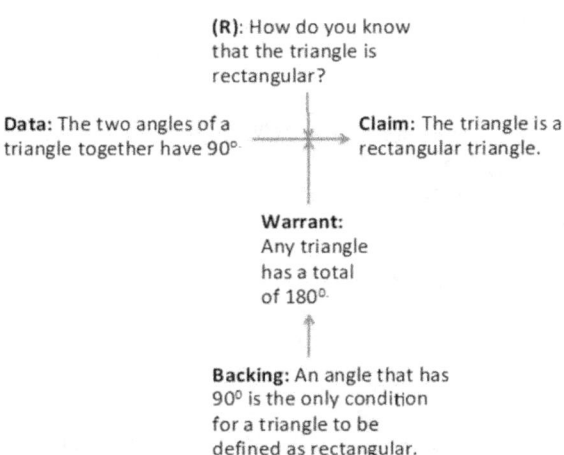

Figure 4.1. *TAP adapted for a deductive argument in Mathematics.*

The second example is from History and it is an inductive argument. The burden of proof lies in the warrant. This means that if we imagine that an addressee challenges the argument, it is the relation between warrant and claim-data that (s)he will challenge, as shown in Figure 4.2.

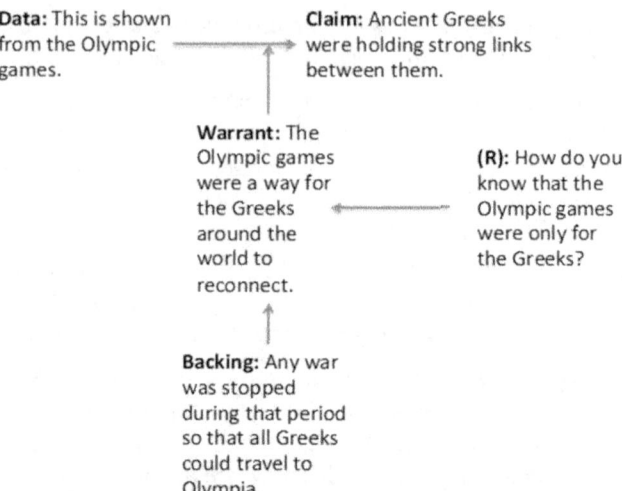

Figure 4.2. *TAP adapted for an inductive argument in History.*

The third example is from Chemistry and it is an abductive argument. In fact, it is the same argument presented in Table 22. The burden of proof lies in the backing. This means that if we imagine that an addressee challenges the argument, it is the relation between claim/data and backing that (s)he will challenge, as shown in Figure 4.3.

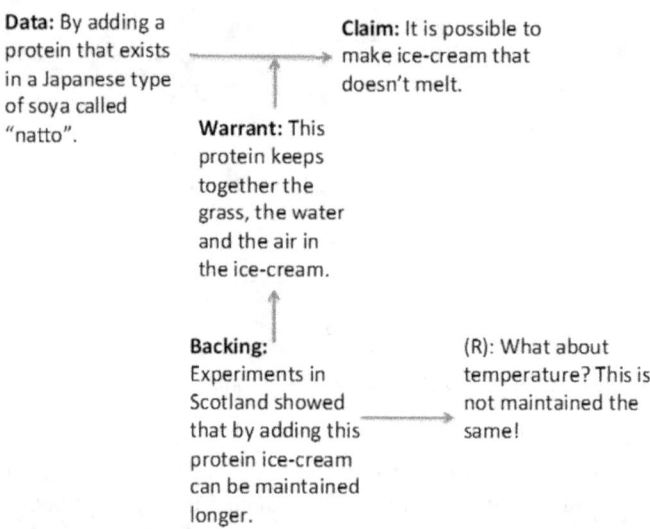

Figure 4.3. *TAP adapted for an abductive argument in Chemistry.*

Concluding remarks

As a conclusion it can be said: Yes, there is field-dependency when it comes to defining what counts as claim, data, warrant, and backing in a specific disciplinary field; and yes, the application of different types of reasoning influences what counts as evidence in each discipline-related argument. However, it is not the disciplinary field itself that defines the difference, but the location of the burden of proof that defines which of the TAP elements used is more probable to be challenged in an imaginary dialogue. This location, expressed as a question in italics in each one of the Figures above, forms the basis of a potential rebuttal (answer to an anticipated challenge or counterargument) related to a particular type of evidence, either warrant or backing.

This remark is very important as it defines how argument-based teaching may be structured in each disciplinary field. As different scientific communities engage in argumentation practices differently (Gray & Kang, 2014), identifying how these discipline-related differences get manifested in argumentative discourse is a pre-condition for effective argument-based teaching to take place. However, among the three main types of reasoning (i.e. deductive, inductive, and abductive), it is abductive reasoning that focuses the critical doubt on the *backing*, thus, the search for genuine evidence is inherent to it. Based on this idea and also on the fact that abductive reasoning is the only one that creates new knowledge (Peirce, 1878), it was recently proposed as the basis for the promotion of argumentation in the classroom for any disciplinary field (Rapanta, 2018).

Chapter 5

Evaluating students' arguments in different fields

Several studies have focused on the impact of argumentative practice on learning how to argue at all educational levels, from primary school to university (e.g. Asterhan & Schwarz, 2016; Mitchell & Andrews, 2000). The case of adolescents is crucial as the development of their argumentative competence mainly depends on the opportunities they are given for arguing. First, they have acquired all the basic developmental skills implied in the human natural capacity to argue, such as the production of justifications and counterarguments, already present by the age of 11 (Mercier, 2011). Second, they are able to apply sophisticated argumentation strategies similar to the ones applied by adults (Felton, 2004). However, studies focusing on adolescents have shown that their manifested argument performance in an "argument-free" classroom environment is low (Driver, Newton, & Osborne, 2000; Kuhn & Crowell, 2011). It is through their exposure to dialogic argumentation that the quality and frequency of students' argumentative discourse increases (Zohar & Nemet, 2002; Kuhn & Udell, 2003).

Examples of pedagogical interventions focusing on argumentation mainly emerge from the field of natural sciences, due to the strong relation between scientific reasoning and argumentation (Duschl, Schweingruber, & Shouse, 2007), as already discussed in Chapter 1. For instance, it has been shown that students practicing argumentation in the science classroom are able to learn complex scientific concepts (Zohar & Nemet, 2002; Hennessey, 2003; Nussbaum & Sinatra, 2003; Nussbaum, Sinatra, & Poliquin, 2008), coordinate between theory and evidence (Chinn & Brewer, 1998; Kuhn, 2002; Osborne, et al., 2004; Lehrer & Schauble, 2005), and adopt scientific epistemological practices (Jimenez-Aleixandre et al., 2000; Osborne et al, 2004; Sandoval, 2005). However, evidence for the positive impact of argument-related activities and argument-based teaching also exists for other disciplinary fields, such as History (e.g. De la Paz & Felton, 2010; De La Paz et al., 2012) or Language Arts (Litman & Greenleaf, 2017; Wilkinson et al., 2017). In addition, the use of socio-scientific issues as a springboard for promoting argumentation practices and skills has also extensively attracted researchers' attention (e.g. Jiménez-Aleixandre & Pereiro-Muñoz, 2002; Erduran et al., 2004; Evagorou & Dillon, 2011).

Because of the positive outcomes of practicing argumentation in the classroom, and of the various educational policy documents emphasizing the development of argument skills among youth (NRC, 1996; NRC, 2007; EU, 2006), several teacher professional development programs focusing on argumentation have been implemented in different parts of the world. In regards to their impact on students' performance, some of the programs can be considered very successful, although others seem to be somewhat ineffective, as Sedova, Sedlacek, and Svaricek (2016) remark. For example, it is, yet, not clear how and whether teacher education programs contribute to the development of critical argumentation skills, as they have been originally defined by Kuhn (1991) as: (a) the skill to construct valid arguments and find the right evidence for them, (b) the skill to construct valid counterarguments or alternative theories and find the right evidence for them, and (c) the skill to construct valid refutations that respond to counterarguments.

As already discussed in Chapter 1, most educational research nowadays that focuses on argumentation, implements Toulmin's Argument Pattern (TAP) as the main method of analysis and assessment (Rapanta et al., 2013). However, the mostly used TAP's adaptations (e.g. Erduran et al., 2004; McNeill, Lizotte, Krajcik, & Marx, 2006) only focus on scientific arguments, leaving out other disciplinary areas. In addition, one of the critiques that TAP has received by educational researchers is the difficulty to distinguish between data, warrants, and backings. Although authors seem to agree that the three elements are all different types of *grounding* or *reasoning* that support the claim (Simon, 2008; Berland & McNeill, 2010), no clear distinctive criteria have been thus far applied with consistency in educational research.

The goal of this chapter is two-fold: first, to propose a coding scheme of critical argumentation adaptable to different contexts; and second, to identify the impact that an argument-based teaching program has on promoting middle-grade classroom argumentation both as a process (pedagogic discourse and practices) and as a product (students' spontaneous arguments).

The focus on critical argumentation through the construction of a coding scheme is crucial in my approach, mainly because existing frameworks of argument quality applied and proposed in educational contexts lack the notion of criticality. On the contrary, the Critical Argumentation Scheme (CAS) proposed in this chapter as a diagnostic tool of students' arguments produced individually takes into consideration the following elements of critical argumentation: (a) the field dependency in defining what counts as an evidence in different disciplinary areas; (b) the distinction between explanation and argumentative support; and (c) the inclusion of relevance as a pre-defining criteria of characterization of any argument element manifested in discourse.

Critical argumentation skills and their promotion

To define critical argumentation skills, the relationship between critical thinking and argumentation needs to be looked at. Critical thinking and argumentation are two terms often encountered together in educational research studies, mainly because argumentation is thought to enhance critical thinking skills, as manifested in students' critical discourse (Osborne, 2010). Hereby, I adopt Walton's (1989) view that critical thinking refers to some general dispositions such as empathy and critical detachment, which are straightforwardly developed through engagement in argumentative dialogue. As Walton (1989) puts it, "the common core of basic critical thinking skills underlying critical reasoning (...) is the *key ability to look at both sides of an argument*. The structure behind this ability is the concept of argument as dialogue" (p. 182, emphasis added).

A critical look at the reality first of all means that the person accepts that reality may have multiple interpretations and that different theories may apply to the same data, and vice versa, which was also defined as "antilogos" (Glassner & Schwarz, 2007). Lack of manifestation of this ability results to two of the main critical thinking flaws, defined as 'my-side' bias and 'makes-sense' epistemology (Perkins, Farady, & Bushey, 1991). I agree with Wolfe and Britt (2008) that my-side bias does not refer to the force with which an author defends his own argument. Following Kuhn (1991), this critical thinking bias refers to the lack of ability of a speaker or a writer to accept the existence and validity of any alternative theories to his/her own. In this sense, being unable to produce any antilogos, subjects are restricted to a rather absolutist epistemological set of beliefs, which are far from the critical or evaluativist stance (Kuhn & Park, 2005). The lack of critical stance also results in the adoption of the first available view or data that "makes sense" without a rigorous analysis of its relevance, sufficiency, and acceptability. Although these quality standards are very much discussed in the informal logic field, their adaptation and implementation in educational research are still scarce.

The present study

The TAPping framework proposed by Erduran et al. (2004), which is currently the most known adaptation of TAP in educational research, fails to address several critical aspects of students' argumentation, as already discussed in Chapter 4. One of these aspects is the field-dependency of the grounds used to support a claim. The need for a generic tool of argument analysis and assessment, adaptable to different disciplinary fields, emerges. Moreover, this tool should be of a diagnostic nature, serving the individual assessment requirements of educational programs worldwide, which place critical thinking and inquiry skills on the spotlight of teaching and learning practices. As such, a focus on the individual argumentation skills manifested critically in a given context is necessary.

Among the studies designed to promote argumentation practices and skills in the classroom, it can be said that there mainly exist two types: the ones based on the intervention designed and implemented by the researchers, and the others based on how trained and/or expert teachers implement argumentative discourse, in the form of dialogue, with their students. As anticipated in the Introduction, this book focuses on this second trend, hereby referred to as argument-based teaching.

Several empirical studies on supporting and assessing teachers' argument-based pedagogical content knowledge (PCK) have been carried out in the last two decades. Here I focus on some examples of studies discussing the impact of teachers' training on their students' argumentation. Erduran et al. (2004) describe a two-year intervention in which 12 junior high school science teachers were taught how to promote students´ argumentation in their classrooms. The posttest showed significant improvements in students´ quality and quantity of arguments produced. In another longitudinal case study reported by Martin and Hand (2009), one elementary science teacher was observed during two years in her efforts to apply an argumentative approach in her classroom. During the second phase of the study, the teacher´s questioning patterns changed, the role of the student voice shifted, and aspects of science argument began to appear. In her case study with five chemistry middle school teachers, McNeill (2009) identified several instructional practices that support students production of claims, evidence and reasoning, such as defining, modeling and critiquing scientific explanations or making the rationale behind scientific explanations explicit.

Although these and few other case studies (e.g. Herrenkohl et al., 1999; Duschl & Osborne, 2002; Dawson & Venville, 2010) shed light on teacher argumentation practices, there is a considerable lack in identifying the connections between the strategies taught, their implementation by the participant teachers, and the impact of their implementation on students' critical argumentation skills. The study presented in this chapter endeavors to fill in this gap through looking at the effects that argument-based teaching has on students' individual manifestations of "criticality" in three different disciplinary areas, namely Science (including Physics and Natural Sciences), History, and Civic Education.

As I wanted to achieve the above goal through the teachers themselves and not through a research-based intervention, I was further interested in identifying: (a) the implementability of the contents and strategies taught and their transfer from the teacher educator class to the actual classroom; and (b) the perceived change from part of the students as participants and main stakeholders in the new, argument-rich environment. Apart from this empirical goal, the present study also serves a methodological goal: that of proposing a rubric of identifying levels of critical argumentation that can be applied in any disciplinary field, but that takes into account the relevance of the argument elements to the subject matter at hand.

The IMPACT project

The qualitative study described here was part of a two-phase exploratory design-based research project on identifying and sustaining argument-based teaching practices in the middle-grades. According to the design-based research paradigm, educational scientists provide insights into the local dynamics, while at the same time they draw connections to theories and theoretical assertions, continuously refining them to produce ontological innovations (Barab & Squire, 2004; DiSessa & Cobb, 2004). The IMPACT project followed this paradigm as the research team closely accompanied the participant teachers since the beginning till the end of the project with the threefold goal of: (a) understanding the existing, if any, dialogue-based pedagogies; (b) suggesting ways of rendering them (more) argument-related; and (c) proposing and adapting the most adequate research instruments to address the problems and questions emerged.

The first phase that took place from September to December 2016 consisted of non-participant observation of 62 class hours (45 minutes each), distributed among ten teachers working in three schools (two public and one private) in the broader area of Lisbon, Portugal. Of these ten, only six voluntarily continued to the second phase, which entailed the actual teacher education course, comprised of 36 in situ and 20 ex-situ (homework and classwork in their own classes) hours. The second phase took place from February to May 2017.

Participants

The present study focuses on four of the six participant teachers, for being the most proactive in designing their own materials and activities. Two of these teachers participated in the same classroom, one teaching Physics and the other Natural sciences. The two remaining teachers participated with one Civic Education and one History class. All four teachers were female, working in two different public schools in Lisbon. Their participation in the project was voluntary, following the consent of the school directors. Parents' informed consent for all the students of the three classrooms was also acquired, through the teachers, before any classroom observation took place.

The total number of students was 90, equally distributed among the three participant classrooms. In Portugal, the middle grades (*terceiro ciclo*) form part of the Basic Education (*Ensino Básico*) but belong to the Secondary Education building and system of teaching (several teachers instead of one). Due to the change of school at the 7th grade, most students face some difficulties of adaptation, which are then overcome in the last two grades of the same cycle. This study's participants were distributed among the 7th and the 9th grades. The average age of the students was 13,7 years old and the percentage of girls and boys was 55% and 45% correspondingly.

Characteristics of the Teacher Professional Development (PD) program

A unique characteristic of the teacher PD program implemented in the study is that it was both *a part* and an *outcome* of the research design followed. On one hand, teachers were involved since the beginning of the year in the argumentation project, without receiving any input (either advice or training) regarding their pedagogical practices at the time. At the same time, the observed classrooms in this initial phase served as a basis for the design of the contents of the teacher course, which took place during four months (February till end of May 2017).

The other unique characteristic of the teacher PD is that it was aiming at teachers from different disciplinary areas. Therefore, it could only address aspects of argument-based teaching that could be transferrable to all contexts (at least each one of the four disciplinary areas involved). For this reason, both the course objectives and contents were generic as it can be seen in Table 23. Special attention was given to the instructional design aspects of argumentation (see Chapter 1), as well as the capacitation of types of dialogue that are more argument-promoting than others (see Chapter 3).

Table 23. Teachers' course objectives and contents.

Course objectives	Contents
Prepare argumentation activities in a structured and efficient way.	Argument-based teaching methods and argumentation strategies; successful tools, activities, and techniques.
Analyze and evaluate written student arguments.	Methods of argument analysis and assessment; structure and quality of written arguments.
Identify when a classroom conversation tends to be argumentative and guide dialogue towards that direction.	Structure and quality of dialogic arguments; argumentation schemes and their use for teaching.

Reflect on one's own teaching practice and on the value of promoting constructive dialogue and argumentation in the classroom.	Argumentation practice in small groups; ideas for argumentation activities and support in their design.

Another main focus of the PD was the identification and dynamization of dialogic argumentation strategies, already present, but in an hybridic form, in the classrooms observed before the training. Teachers manifested several potential dialogic strategies, most of them of a Socratic inquiry nature, but very few of them had naturally engaged their students in more genuine argumentative interactions, such as discovery and persuasion dialogues. The PD focused on identifying and showcasing some potentially argumentative dialogic sequences of the pre-training classrooms and guiding reflection on how those sequences could improve in terms of their argumentative quality. This was defined in terms of both arguments-as-products, implementing Toulmin's elements to identify arguments enacted in dialogic discourse, and arguments-as-processes, adapting Walton's types of argumentation dialogue to the classroom dialogue context.

All teachers participating in the PD program received a rubric of self-evaluation of their own argument-related goals and guidelines on how to pursue them. The rubric was based on a recent project on dialogic teaching held in the United States (Reznitskaya & Wilkinson, 2017), as part of which the Argumentation Rating Tool (ART) was developed (Reznitskaya et al., 2016). I adapted this tool as a self-assessment rubric since the beginning of the project, so that the participant teachers would be able to record their own strategies that promote students' critical argumentation throughout the program, as well as any changes in their use of such strategies. They were also asked to use their notes on that rubric in their self-evaluation reports that they delivered in order to receive accreditation for their participation at the end of the program. Examples of the manifestation of the dialogic teaching elements in the self-evaluation reports were given in Chapter 1.

Data collection

Two different datasets were constructed as emerged from: (a) students' written arguments at the beginning and towards the end of the school year, and (b) students' interviews in regards to the usefulness of argument-based teaching as perceived by them throughout the project. Teachers' self-evaluation reports regarding their implementation of argumentation strategies based on ART, as explained above, were also used as a complementary source.

Students' written responses

The sample of the students' texts that formed part of the analysis consisted of a total of 168 texts, divided into 82 pre-implementation and 86 post-implementation texts (for convenience I will henceforth refer to them as pretest and posttest texts although the design of the study was not experimental). By implementation I mean the application of argumentation strategies and activities by the participant teachers in their classrooms. Table 24 shows the distribution of texts per classroom and per phase. The total number of texts produced at both phases was 170.

Table 24. Number of texts produced per classroom at each one of the two phases.

Classrooms	Pretest	Posttest	Total
Natural sciences	30	28	58
Civic education	24	29	53
History	28	29	57
Total	82	86	168

All texts that formed part of this study were students' free answers to an argumentative question related to the contents taught in each one of the classrooms. For the question selection, teachers had to make sure that it was open enough to include various aspects and justifications of the same issue, thus not directing students to only one correct answer, but leaving open the space of argumentative inquiry, to be manifested in their writing. As for the topics, these had to be of general interest, so that homogenized results across disciplines could be obtained. Applying these criteria, all participant teachers came up with two issues-questions each, of comparable nature and difficulty, according to them. Figure 5.1 presents a list of the questions-issues selected by the teachers for each one of the three classrooms, with some necessary contextual clarifications. The average time for the production of the texts in all classrooms was 15 minutes, and no word limit was provided. After each writing production phase, teachers collected the texts written by hand on blank sheets and immediately gave them to the researcher. No discussion or reference was ever made to the first-phase texts in order not to influence the second-phase written products.

Class	Pre-implementation writing task	Post-implementation writing task
Science	At the end of one class about Mediterranean diet and its main components, the teacher asked students to write and adequately justify their opinion about the following question: "The Mediterranean diet is recommended by many nutritionist scientists as one which promotes a healthy life. Do you agree with this?"	The topic was 'adolescence' and more precisely how the body changes relate to adolescents' feeling of suffering. The teacher used a song as a trigger for the activity and more precisely a lyric saying: "everything around is ugly, I just feel like escaping". Then she asked students to write and justify their opinion about the feeling of suffering as related to adolescence, having in mind the body changes discussed.
Civic Education	The teacher first gave to all students a copy of the rights and duties of students inside the school and also some based on the general status of the student, which is an official document that students are supposed to know when starting the school. She then asked them to choose one right and one duty that they consider as the most important and justify their selection.	The topic was 'family'. Students sat in groups choosing who is representing which member of a family. This was to prepare the group activity that followed. Before that, they were asked to choose and answer one out of a list of proposed questions: "Do we have to trust our families?", "Is it better to have siblings, or be the only child?", "Is it always good to be in family?", etc.
History	The teacher gave the students the following statement and asked them to write their opinion and justify it based on the information in the manual. The statement was: "The participation of Portugal in the First World War served the interests of the first Republic".	The teacher first proposed a ludic activity in dyads, for which students had to complete the bubbles of a cartoon, arguing in favor and against the Portuguese regime of 1974, year in which the Colonial War was ended with the Carnation Revolution of the 25th April. Right after, students had to write and justify their opinion individually about the statement: "The revolution of 25th April 1974 established a democratic regime and proposed a solution for the Colonial War, which essentially resulted in conceding the Portuguese citizenship to the colonies' native population".

Figure 5.1. *The argumentative questions/issues selected by the teachers in the three classrooms.*

Students' interviews

To further investigate any impact of the teacher-training program on students' argumentation, a semi-structured interview was implemented focusing on the positive and negative outcomes that the argument-based teaching had on the students, as perceived by them. The interview questions were open and did not focus directly on the argumentation skills manifested by the students as a result of the argument-based teaching. They were rather inviting students to reflect on any change they had possibly perceived regarding their own oral and writing performance in general throughout the course, as result of the argumentative discussions and activities they engaged with during their classes.

The interviews' goal was to better understand whether any positive change remarked in the individual argument oral (classroom participation) and written performance could be considered as an effect of argument-based teaching. Therefore, I chose to focus the interviews on those students who, according to their teachers, benefitted the most from this type of teaching. The sample of the interviewed students, although not randomly selected, was representative in terms of their academic performance and learning capacities. In total, 30 students (14 boys and 16 girls) were interviewed by the author, with whom they were already familiar from the observed lessons. The interviewees' participation was on a voluntary basis (after teachers' invitation) and it was equally distributed among the three classrooms. All interviews were fully transcribed.

Data analysis methods

For the analysis of the transcribed interviews, I used the inductive content analysis method (Elo & Kyngäs, 2008). Further information regarding the analysis of the interviews is given in the Findings section. For the identification of levels of critical argumentation in students' written arguments, I constructed the CAS coding scheme described below.

The Critical Argumentation Scheme (CAS)

For the analysis of students' written arguments, a coding scheme based on TAP elements was proposed. The scheme is similar to the one proposed by Erduran et al. (2004) in two aspects: first, both consist of five levels; second, warrants and backings are considered of equal importance. However, in Erduran et al. (2004) framework data are also considered of equal importance to warrants and backings, although in the CAS they are not. The CAS further differentiates itself from existing schemes in proposing four criteria, which, according to the author, are akin to grasp the critical thinking aspects of argumentative discourse. These are the following:

> **C1.** The more supported an argument by warrants and/or backings, the higher the level of critical argumentation; the use of warrants and backings to support arguments shows a high level of epistemic awareness and an understanding of the goal to persuade an audience providing as much evidence as possible (Sandoval & Millwood, 2005; Macagno, 2016).
>
> **C2.** The more consideration is given towards the 'other side' of one's own argument, through counterarguments and rebuttals, the higher the level of critical argumentation; the integration of alternative or contrary theories in one own's discourse shows an understanding of the evaluative nature of argumentation (Kuhn & Udell, 2003; Erduran et al., 2004).
>
> **C3.** The more explanation is used as a substitute for warrants and backings, the lower the level of critical argumentation (Kuhn, 1991; Brem & Rips, 2000); and

C4. The more irrelevant information is integrated into any of the argument elements, the lower the level of critical argumentation (Sandoval, 2003; Schwarz et al., 2003; Macagno, 2016).

The four criteria and the rationale for their selection are presented in Figure 5.2.

Criteria of performance	Effect on critical argumentation	Rationale
C1: Presence of support (warrants and backings).	Positive (Sandoval & Millwood, 2005; Macagno, 2016).	The use of warrants and backing to support arguments shows a high level of epistemic awareness and an understanding of the goal to persuade an audience providing as much evidence as possible.
C2: Considering the 'other side', i.e. including counter-arguments and rebuttals.	Positive (Kuhn & Udell, 2003; Erduran et al., 2004).	The integration of alternative or contrary theories in one's own discourse shows an understanding of the evaluative nature of argumentation. Moreover, the presence of rebuttals is a significant indicator of the quality of argumentation, as rebuttals force students to evaluate the validity and strength of their own arguments.
C3: Use of explanation instead of grounding.	Negative (Brem & Rips, 2000).	When used as stand-alone grounding instead of warrants or backings, explanations are counter-productive, as they equal to what Kuhn (1991) defined as *pseudo-evidence*, i.e. non-valid justification of one's position.
C4: Use of irrelevant information.	Negative (Sandoval, 2003; Schwarz et al, 2003; Macagno, 2016).	Any information needs to be relevant both to the topic and to the structure of the argument discourse, otherwise it might be misleading or weaken the argument.

Figure 5.2. *Criteria used for the construction of the CAS scheme.*

An innovative element of CAS is the distinction between data, further support, and explanation. For an argument to be constructed, a claim plus data is necessary. This data refers to the first available evidence used to support a claim. Thus, defining what counts as data is a natural consequence of defining what counts as a claim in each disciplinary area. For general interest and socio-scientific topics, usually expressed in the form of dilemmas, the claim is related to taking position A or B, as for example agreeing or not with the capital punishment (Kuhn, 1991) or with the construction of a new zoo (Erduran et al., 2004). In a Civic Education class, claims may also take the form of a value claim, as for example comparing one citizen's right to another by stating which one is the most important. In science, claims are statements that express an aspect of a manifestation of a phenomenon. In History, claims are statements that express a value of a historical event. This value might relate either to how true (accurate, complete) the statement is, or to how an event may be assessed (importance, positive/negative, etc.).

Although what counts as a claim might differ from area to area and from topic to topic, the function of the data is always the same, i.e. to support the claim in ways that together, data and claim may form a disputable opinion or a personal theory about a particular issue. In summary, the data, or grounds, correspond to "whatever detailed assemblage of facts, observations, statistical data, previous conclusions, or other specific information" a person relies on "as the immediate support for his specific claim" (Toulmin, Rieke, & Janik, 1984; p. 38).

If data corresponds to a first-level *what-explanation*, then warrant forms part of what can be called the *reason-explanation*. According to Toulmin (1958), data are "the facts we appeal to as a foundation for the claim", whereas warrants are the "general, hypothetical statements, which can act as bridges" between the data and the claim (p. 91). Educational researchers have interpreted warrants differently. For instance, according to Sampson and Clark (2008), "warrants are comments that are used to justify why data are relevant to the claim" (451). According to Bell and Linn (2000), warrants may distinguish "argument explanations" from "descriptive explanations". However, it is not clear how warrant is different than the backing: "Backings are used in arguments to substantiate warrants in explanation" (ibid, p. 804).

To avoid this confusion between warrant, backing, and explanation, CAS distinguishes between *support*, when warrants or other secondary evidence (backings) are used to support an argument, and *explanation*, when another type of support rather than evidence-based knowledge is used to support an argument. This distinction is also rooted in the idea that when used as stand-alone grounding instead of warrants and backings, explanations are counterproductive, as they equal to what Kuhn (1991) defined as pseudo-evidence, i.e. non-valid justification of one's position. On the contrary, when explanations are used together with valid justifications, i.e. warrants and/or backings, may add value to the argument (Mayes, 2010; Osborne & Patterson, 2011).

When it comes to critical argumentation, looking at the other side of one's own argument is an essential part, as explained earlier. The only TAP element that reveals the critical thinking skill of antilogos is the rebuttal. Toulminian rebuttals were described as assertions that contradict the claim or represent exceptions to the claim. In this sense, rebuttal is nearer to a counterargument included in one's own argumentative reasoning chain. However, for someone to be skilled in critical argumentation, forming counterarguments is not enough: first, they need to make sure that they are valid, finding the right backing and/or warrants to support them; second they need to be able to reply to such implicit or explicit counterarguments in ways that refute their strength, and thus give more strength to one's initial claim (Kuhn, 1991). According to Leitão (2000), replies to counterarguments might also take different forms rather than the rebuttal, such as: dismissal, local agreement, integrative reply, or withdrawal of the initial view. In this study, as the focus is on critical argumentation as expressed in written texts, I propose a TAP-based redefinition of rebuttal as a dismissive, undercutting, or integrative "reply" to an explicitly considered counterargument.

Last but not least, CAS also considers "irrelevant information" as a separate discourse category. Relevance is an important aspect in argument construction and assessment, mainly related to the use of evidence (Macagno, 2016). Therefore, the use of relevant information in one's arguments and counterarguments is a sign of critical argumentation skills. All previously mentioned argument elements, including explanations, were coded as such only when they were considered relevant to (a) the topic/issue of argumentation and (b) the internal structure of the discourse. On the contrary, a discourse element was coded as "irrelevant" when it was either uninformative or incoherent (Macagno, 2016). Table 25 shows examples of each one of the CAS elements.

Table 25. Examples of coded discourse in two students' texts.

Text 1	Code
Throughout adolescence, adolescents undergo various changes in the body, both, exterior and interior, these body changes may be related to the sense of suffering	Claim
because the teenager may not feel good about himself and his/her "new" body.	Data
The teenager may suffer, because he or she may be bullied, hacked or de-meant by his/ her peers and this may be associated with his or her changes.	Warrant/Backing
There are people who deal well with these changes	Counterargument
but others who do not deal in the same way.	Rebuttal
Text 2	**Code**
I do not know; I do not have any pain.	Irrelevant
In my opinion, it does not make a teenager suffer	Claim
rather he/she may be astonished or afraid of what will happen	Claim
but he/she will never have any pain unless he/she falls in love.	Claim

The texts above were produced by two different classmates as an answer to the same question regarding whether adolescence is related to a sense of suffering, as a part of the body changes (see Data collection section). Text 1 has a complete, partially two-sided argument structure, as it misses any support (warrants or backings) for the counterargument. On the contrary, Text 2 does not even include a basic argument as it only contains three claims and an irrelevant statement in the beginning. The relevance of the three claims themselves is also doubtful as they relate only to one part of the topic (suffering) without addressing the body changes.

Each text produced by the students was given a final code based on the combination of the CAS elements present. For example, a text containing one claim, two data, one backing, one warrant, and one counterargument was coded as "C1D2S2CA1". On the basis of these codes, the critical argumentation level manifested in each text was decided based on the CAS rubric presented on Table 26. According to this rubric, the same code above would correspond to a Level 4 argument.

Table 26. Coding scheme for critical argumentation (CA) levels.

CA level	Description
Level 0	No argument.
Level 1	At least one claim (C) supported by at least one data (D); Level 2 texts that contain at least one piece of irrelevant information (II) are de-graded to this level.
Level 2	At least one claim (C) supported by at least one data (D) further supported by one type of "support" (S), either backing or warrant, or accompanied by one counterargument (CA).
Level 3	At least one claim (C) supported by at least one data (D), and further supported by more than one "supports" (S), either backings or warrants or counterarguments (CA).
Level 4	At least one claim (C) supported by at least one data (D) and support (S), accompanied by at least one counterargument (CA).
Level 5	At least one claim (C) supported by at least one data (D) and support (S), accompanied by at least one counterargument (CA) and one support for the counterargument (CAS) or by one rebuttal (R).
Level 6	At least one claim (C) supported by at least one data (D) and support (S), accompanied by at least one counterargument (CA) and one support for the counterargument (CAS) and one rebuttal (R).

Note: Explanations (E) when present did not influence the coding of levels, but they were distinguished from Support (S), which is a necessary element for Levels 2-6.

All texts were coded by the author and a research assistant who was trained to the coding scheme and acted as a blind rater. The inter-rater reliability for the CAS levels was 87% (Cohen's Kappa=0.80).

Findings

From 'argument-free' to 'argument-based' teaching

In order to verify whether the three teachers implemented the learnt argument-based teaching strategies their classroom's discourse before the training was compared to their classroom's discourse after the training. To do that, I focused on the TAP-based argument moves made by all participants in each selected class. Table A1 in the Appendix shows an example of coded classroom discourse based on Toulmin's argument elements.

I then focused only on student moves and I rated as "1" all claim and data moves, as "2" all warrant and backing moves, and as "3" all counterargument and rebuttal moves. This allowed me to identify the level of student-generated argument explicitness for each class. I then performed a Mann-Whitney U Test for the pre-training and the post-training rating scores for each class. For the History class, the result was significant at $p < .05$ for one-tailed hypothesis, giving a Z-score of -2.74416 ($p = .00307$). For the Natural Science class, the result was significant at $p < .05$ for one-tailed hypothesis, giving a Z-score of 2.47147 ($p = .00676$). Finally, for the Civic Education class, the result was also significant at $p < .05$ for one-tailed hypothesis, giving a Z-score of -1.64965 ($p = .04947$).

Overall, it was shown that the teachers' changed the way they were doing the class, as they allowed space for more students' argumentation to emerge in all three cases. This result was confirmed by the teachers' self-evaluation reports, in which all four argument-based teaching criteria described by Reznitskaya and Wilkinson (2017) were present (see Chapter 1).

From non-critical to critical arguments

Students' texts

As the two types of texts were produced on different dates, not all students produced both types; it was possible that students did not assist both classes during which the teachers asked for the texts to be produced. However, 80 out of the 89 participant students produced both "pre-training" and "post-training" types of texts. Table 27 shows the total frequencies for each one of the seven levels (0-6) between the pre- and the post-training implementation.

Table 27. Pre/post frequencies of texts assessed at each level.

Levels	Pre-training	Post-training
Level 0	6	6
Level 1	38	18
Level 2	16	23
Level 3	13	15
Level 4	3	7
Level 5	2	9
Level 6	2	2

Note: In grey-scale the categories that differ between the pre and post phases.

A Wilcoxon sign-ranked test was applied to the level scores obtained by the students before and after the training (for the detailed pre- and posttest coding for each student see Table A2 in the Appendix). The result was significant at $p < .05$ ($p = .00328$ for a two-tailed hypothesis). Moreover, as the Z-value obtained was negative ($Z = -2.9421$), it can be further confirmed that the change in performance between the two phases was positive. Said otherwise, the students' critical argumentation level results obtained at the post-training phase were significantly better than the results of the pre-training phase.

Students' interviews

The 30 texts obtained by the transcribed students' interviews were analyzed separately by the author and her research assistant, who did the coding independently. The percentage of agreement was 86,6%. The following 47 categories emerged from the compared coding: "participation", "give opinion", "defend opinion", "important for jobs", "prove an idea", "counterargue/search for counterarguments", "improve in the tests/grades", "reply to development questions", "ground/justify an idea", "use in other courses/years", "necessary to do more", "search for arguments/theories", "oral discourse", "written discourse", "persuade", "express oneself", "general knowledge", "use of facts/scientific knowledge", "social/open issues", "groupwork", "explain to colleagues", "learn/understand", "feeling important", "worksheets", "reach a conclusion", "everyday argumentation", "speak in public", "see others' opinions", "respect/listen to others", "different opinions", "presentations", "be more attentive", "task diversity", "funny", "feeling integrated", "structure discourse", "social relations", "reflect/question", "think on both sides of an issue", "role-playing", "invite to talk", "shyness", "take seriously", "confusion", "group structure", "level of difficulty", and "time limit".

At the second level of analysis, we defined some more general categories to include the sub-categories presented above. These were: "utility", "social interaction", "personal development", "critical argumentation skills", "activities", and "challenges". As students' answers showed, they were conscious of the change in terms of their own argumentation skills and how these improved as a result of the argumentation strategies and activities implemented by their teachers.

The most emerging critical argumentation skill as perceived by the students was their enhanced ability to counterargue and think on both sides of an issue. One of the students from the Natural Sciences classroom said:

> "I felt improving my argument competency, achieving to think also how to rebut the arguments that they might present against me, and having a more global vision about the issue on which we argue" (Male, 15 years old; this and the following excerpts were translated from Portuguese).

This was also true for the younger Civic education students. One of them said:

> "(Argumentation) is important for us to understand what the others think and not only what we think that it is the cause (of a problem), and to obtain a better idea about what happens because everyone has their experiences and talk about things that we learn from" (Female, 12 years old).

As far as History students are concerned, learning how to think with counterarguments, as result of the argumentation activities that teachers proposed, was also one of the most important aspects. Nonetheless, some of them made clear that it was not as much about being against someone, rather being attentive to what others said and trying to search for evidence different than theirs:

> "The fact that we were not supposed to repeat others' ideas, but we had to prove what others said, who was right, I think this was the most interesting part of arguing as it allowed us to think not only from our own shoes, to look at both sides of things, and sometimes even more than the two sides; it gave us a way to arrive at different opinions, and understand that sometimes an opinion has different conclusions, more or less" (Female, 14 years old).

The ability to look at and integrate others' opinions was, as expected, also accompanied by the ability to better present and defend one's own argument. This ability was composed of different skills, mentioned by the students, such as: the avoidance of repeating the same data and the search for new evidence, the need to strengthen as much as possible one's position, the need to be clear and relevant. Here are some excerpts of the interviews that provide evidence for the above:

> "I think it was also important that we had to defend an opinion that was given to us, and it was possible that we did not really agree with it. Not only did I learn how to defend my own opinion, but also if I were asked to defend another opinion, (I know that) I have to search for a way to defend that opinion (...) above all, I have to prove what I am saying" (Female, 14 years old).

> "In the past, when I had to present and justify my opinion, I used to repeat a lot, without achieving to organize my arguments, and now, maybe, my arguments are more explicit" (Male, 14 years old).

> "(I learnt how to) use more facts when I argue, not only one or two, but try to find as much (evidence) as possible, and if I find errors in the facts I have or in my argument, try to make the argument stronger" (Male, 14 years old).

Other skills emerged as important from students' first contact with argumentation, which we categorized as "social" and "personal development" skills. Although these skills did not relate directly to the analysis of written argumentation performed, I think it is important to briefly include them here as they form an essential part of the critical disposition developed during early adolescence. Also, they related to the emotional aspects of argumentation, which recent research shows that are important for its development and manifestation (Schwarz & Baker, 2016). Among these aspects, we distinguished the skill to express oneself in public, the skill to collaborate with people other than your friends, and some initial leadership skills (as most of the argumentation activities were related to group work and group representation by one person, usually different each time). It is also important to note that the majority of this type of ideas emerged among the seventh graders, who were the most emotionally exposed due to the new school environment, as explained in the Participants section. Here is some evidence for that:

"Usually I speak at a low voice in front of the class, now I speak louder, and in the role-playing activity we did with the teacher, I was the best" (Female, 13 years old).

"I improved my way of debating, showing what I have to say, my arguments, interacting better with my classmates" (Male, 12 years old).

"I felt loved, acknowledged, because it was as if I were the best, but I am not the best, I think that all of us when we were forced a bit we did well, for that I felt a bit 'bigger' when they chose me as representative" (Female, 14 years old).

Although much work has been done in the field of argumentation concerning well-structured interventions to enhance students' critical thinking and writing skills, we addressed the gap of studying the impact of teachers-led argumentation activities as result of a brief professional development (PD) program. Both the analysis of students' texts and interviews showed that even a brief PD focusing on argumentation strategies to be adopted in any everyday curriculum is impactful on the manifestation of critical argumentation skills in early adolescence. Moreover, we believe that teaching 'argumentatively' is more sustainable than any research interventions that usually take a lot of time from the classes and address specific curriculum needs. Developing more teacher PD programs focusing on generic, cross-disciplinary aspects of argumentation dialogue is a possible proposal emerging from this work. As teachers become more empowered and autonomous in their own implementation of argumentative discourse, reasoning, and dialogue, they benefit a larger number of students throughout the years and in a more efficient, direct manner.

Future work will consist of further analysing the discursive strategies that the PD participants implement in their classrooms and their correlations with the argument discourse elements produced by the students either orally or in written assignments. This would allow for a refinement of the pedagogical content knowledge that teachers need to be able to successfully promote argumentation in their classrooms.

Chapter 6

Some practical implications for argument-based teaching

In this last chapter, some practice-based guidelines will be offered as initial path-makers for educators interested in implementing argument-based teaching in their classrooms. Although they are not exhaustive, they are essential in stimulating and promoting argumentation dialogue in any classroom.

Identifying an issue

The issue is a necessary pre-requisite for any argumentation to take place, either in oral or in written form. The issue is different than a topic, for which there needs to be a doubt or disagreement about it. In this sense, any topic can be transformed into an issue, as long as there is some vagueness or confrontation about it. The other main pre-requisite for argumentation to take place is the need to defend that issue "in front" of an audience. Audience can be either physical or imaginary, as in the case of written argumentation.

When it comes to arguing in the classroom, an issue is that everyone (teacher and students) is interested in finding out more about in order to resolve a doubt and/or disagreement. This resolving needs to be collaborative in terms of shared intention and co-construction, as explained below in the section on Framing. The focus is on the issue, not on the person: everyone involved has equal right to participate in the discussion.

An issue can be translated as the main triggering question for argumentation to take place. It can be of different types, such as: take a decision about A or B; solve a problem; decide which is the best explanation/decision for a problem; find out more about a problem or solution.

When it comes to argument-based teaching, issues can be distinguished between: real issues, and made-up issues. Real issues refer to unresolved problems, also called ill-defined problems; they are real because they really need to be solved. Most of them are of a general nature, treating real-life problems, or of a socio-scientific nature, treating social issues that need some scientific knowledge to be resolved. Real issues usually do not form part of the formal curricula. Thus they need to be introduced as extra-curricular topics/activities. From the examples presented in the Appendix, the activity created by the Civic Education teacher may be considered a real issue, as it treats a definition (What is a family?), and definitions are considered argumentative issues since Aristotle. Examples of socio-scientific issues, often used in argumentation and education research, are: What can we do to reduce pollution? Is the re-use of materials better than recycling? Should zoos exist?, etc.

Made-up issues refer to transforming given contents into issues. For teachers to be able to give life to such issues, they must re-construct science or "camouflage" given knowledge. And for that, they need to focus on the scientific process as being a continuous negotiation between different theories proposed to explain certain facts. This is particularly important in Science, for reasons discussed in Chapter 2. Examples of made-up issues from Physics are presented in Table 28, together with an explanation (in italics) of the part of knowledge that needs to become "unknown" for the issue to make sense.

Table 28. Examples of made-up issues from Science.

Why do objects fall?	*(we pretend) we don't know the gravity law*
Why do objects fall on Earth and fly on other planets?	*(we pretend) we don't know how gravity law works*
How come a magnet is stronger than Earth?	*(we pretend) we don't know the relation between magnetism and gravity*

When it comes to History, real issues may be identified when there are many factors influencing over a question, without yet history identifying, or with historians still disagreeing about, which one is the most predominant. An example of such an issue may be "Why did Hitler hate Jews?". Other types of real history-related issues resemble the socio-scientific issues discussed above, in the sense that they require some moral reasoning. Examples of those real issues are: If Nazism had such negative effects, why do neo-Nazi groups exist? Should Greece have gotten out of the European Union?

Made-up issues are also possible in History. In that case, a teacher's strategy may be the one of asking students to argue about statements that are not correct, either because they are vague, or because they are partially verified according to recognized sources. Statement 1 in Table 29 presents an example of the former, whereas Statement 2 is an example of the latter (the first example also forms part of the Historical argumentation activity presented in the Appendix; both examples were created by one of the History teachers participating in the Project).

Table 29. Examples of "made-up" issues in History.

"Vagueness" example (also see the Appendix)	During the cold war there were alternately conflict phases and calming stages.
"Partially correct information" example	The revolution of 25th April 1974 established a democratic regime and proposed a solution for the Colonial War, which essentially resulted in conceding the Portuguese citizenship to the colonies' native population.

When it comes to Language and Arts, issues may be related to the interpretation of artifacts created by others. The distinction between "real" and "made-up" does not apply here, as anything that might bare a different interpretation might be considered an issue. Examples are: How can you tell that these texts are written by Camões? What do you think the heroes of the story should do/have done regarding X? Do you agree with the author's claim that Y?

Distinguishing between explanation and argument

The great majority of the questions teachers ask are information-seeking or explication questions, rather than questions that trigger argument and critical thinking. Explication questions are of the form "what happened" or "what do you know about X"; whereas explanation questions ask students about "why" or "how" a phenomenon works or an event takes place (Benedict-Chambers et al., 2017). For argumentation dialogue to be triggered, explanation questions may be an initial choice. However, the transformation of explication into explanation questions is not straightforward as shown in Table 30.

Table 30. Transforming explication into explanation questions.

Explication questions	Explanation questions
What types of volcanic eruptions do exist and what is the difference between them?	Why did flashes come out with the eruption of the volcano Sakurajima?
Which were the principal goals of the Society of Nations created in 1919?	Europe fell into a serious economic crisis until 1925. Why did the Society of Nations not achieve to fulfill its goals?
Which are the variables that make an object float instead of sink?	Why do some materials float on the water no matter what their shape, but others float when in one shape and sink in another?

Although explanation questions open up the dialogue and reflection space more than the explication questions, not all the answers received may be of argumentative nature. This is because the communicative act of "giving reasons" may take two very distinct forms: one is "giving explanations" and the other is "giving arguments".

Before continuing with the distinction, let's return to the definition of argument previously stated in the Introduction: an argument is "a set of claims in which one or more of them –the premises- are put forward so as to offer reasons for another claim, the conclusion" (Govier, 2014; p. 1). Simply put, although explaining is about giving reasons, most of them of a causal (e.g. The car accident took place, because vehicle A crashed into vehicle B) or personal nature (e.g. I didn't eat anything today, because I didn't want to), arguing is about stating premises, e.g. statements that will support a claim or a conclusion, in the sense of making it more believable or plausible. Table 31 shows some distinction between explanation and argumentation, both perceived as acts of "giving reasons about X".

Table 31. Distinguishing between explanation and argumentation.

Explanation	Argumentation
Knowledge is not necessary (e.g. sometimes testimony is enough).	Knowledge is necessary (either prior or "obtained" at the moment e.g. through given pieces of evidence).
The goal is to clarify.	The goal is to prove a point over another.
The reasons given are not enough to allow an external critic to judge whether the claim being explained is true or not.	The reasons given are open and available to be tested, so that a critic may judge whether the claim is defended in a relevant, sufficient, and acceptable manner.

The distinction between explanation and argumentation is necessary for reasons of evaluation and scaffolding. When assessing students' arguments, for example, "explaining" reasons should be distinguished from "justifying" reasons. To make this distinction, educators may apply the two questions proposed by Kuhn (2001), already discussed in Introduction, being: "How do you know that x?" and "Why do you say so?". I would add a third question here, "What do you mean by x?", and I will explain right away why.

Explanations have a special place in Science, as they form part of the arguments put forward. When students are asked to explain a phenomenon, they are making a claim providing the necessary data to support it, in other words, they come up with a theory, based on some evidence. This "theory plus evidence" may be a first answer to the question "How do you know that phenomenon X takes place?". For example, in a Science classroom about planting, after students have conducted their experiments testing different variables such as light, water, and soil, a group of students may come up with the claim that "Plants die because of lack of light". Then, to the teacher's question "How do you know it is because of that?", they must bring out the evidence obtained from their experiments, meaning the observations carried out during a period of time. An answer, for example, might be: "We know that because of the four plants we had only plant C survived, and it was the only one that received enough light". This is a scientific explanation used to support the theoretical claim "Plants die because of lack of light". Students may be asked to further back up their theory through making explicit their reasoning with the question "Why do say that it was because of light that plant C survived?". To that question, students are expected to reveal all their further observations about how variables were related in their experiment, which allowed them to come up to that conclusion. This will be the "reasoning" phase from the Claim-Evidence-Reasoning framework proposed within the science inquiry curricula (see Chapter 4).

Nonetheless, in other learning contexts, the natural sequence of the questions mentioned above will be: "Why do you say so?" (as an explanation question triggering argumentation dialogue), "How do you know that X" (as an evidence-seeking question), and "What do you mean by that?" (as a clarification question posed either for the explanation or the evidence given). An example will be given from a Literature class in which the teacher asks students to identify which parts of a given text reveal that it is written by a known author X. A student may reply that it is in certain paragraphs/lines and (s)he will nominate them. That will be the claim. Then the teacher may further ask which exact words (s)he is based on to come up to the conclusion that these parts are written by author X. That will be the question "Why do you say so?" asking for the concrete data, exact words used by the author. Once done, the teacher may ask for further evidence, leading the student to establish connections between the studies made about the writing style of that particular author and the manifestation of this style in that words or phrases (s)he mentioned. That will be the evidence part (warrant and backing).

In the examples above, it is clear that explanations form part of the argumentative reasoning, as a first level of giving reasons. When it comes to oral argumentation, the questions mentioned above may be used as prompts for eliciting either these "first-level" reasons or further backing of those and their relation with the claim. However, when it comes to written argumentation, it is common that students mix up different types and levels of reasons, not being clear when they refer to existing data or when they differentiate evidence from their use and interpretation of it (see also Berland and Reiser, 2009). Moreover, it is also common that they tend to explain facts by adding more information about them, which would be a reply to an imaginary "What do you mean by that" question. Although this information giving is important for clarifying meanings, it certainly does not add to the argument quality of students' products. It is this type of "explanation" as clarifying data that forms part of the Critical Argumentation Scheme (Chapter 5), but does not add (neither takes) any value to the arguments produced.

Framing the activity

An important part of teachers' role in promoting argumentation is framing the epistemic activities that take part at each moment of the class. Framing is answering the question "What kind of activity is going on here?". Research suggests that there is a need for explicit cues from the part of the teachers, each time an epistemic activity changes. For example, when a teacher introduces an argumentation activity, the goals of such activity need to be made explicit to the students. Another type of framing consists of asking students to explain their answers. This is very important, and it might also consist a kind of "meta-framing", as teachers are allowed to identify any mismatching in students' perception of the epistemic activity or teachers' framing of the activity.

If framing is conceived as a manifestation of teachers' communicative intentions, we can easily understand that not all framing is productive from an argumentation point of view. A characteristic example is the Initiation-Response-Evaluation (IRE) framework of classroom discourse, first described by Mehan (1979). A simple move from the teacher's part may be enough for communicating his/her intention as being the one of assessing students' answers are good or bad, instead of acknowledging them, which is a necessary pre-requisite for opening up the dialogue space. The comparison of two simple dialogue sequences proposed by Mehan (1979) showcases this difference in intention, as shown in Table 32.

Table 32. The "What time is it, Denise" dialogue example (Mehan, 1979).

Speaker	Acknowledging pattern	IRE pattern
A	What time is it, Denise?	What time is it, Denise?
B	2:30.	2:30.
A	*Thank you, Denise.*	*Very well, Denise.*

Although the well-known IRE pattern on its own does not allow space for reflection, exploration, and eventually argumentation (see also Lemke, 1990), there exist alterations of it that may manifest a different teacher's communicative intention than merely the one of assessing students' knowledge in the sense of a cross-examination. A "simple" alteration of the IRE pattern regards the substitution of the last move, usually performed by the teacher, by a Follow-up move, which would turn the IRE pattern into an Initiation-Response-Follow-up (IRF) sequence (Wells, 1993). This follow-up move, performed by the teacher, may take different forms such as: recapitulations (i.e. summarizing and reviewing what has gone before); elicitations (i.e. asking a question designed to stimulate recall); repetitions (i.e. repeating a student's answer, either to acknowledge it or to encourage an alternative); reformulations (i.e. paraphrasing a student's answer, to make it more accessible to the rest of the class, or to improve the way it has been expressed); and exhortations (i.e. encouraging students to "think" or "remember" what has been said or done earlier)[3].

The transformation of the IRE pattern discussed above is only at an exchange level of discourse. Differences in the teacher's communicative intention can also be manifested at a sequence level. These differences may be either initiated by the teacher or by the students. Mortimer and Scott (2003) suggest two interaction patterns to be added to the traditional IRE (or IRF) pattern. One is a closed chain of interactions, in which the initiation by the teacher may generate different responses from the students, followed up by teacher prompts (P) to generate further responses. The sequence, which is finally closed down with an evaluation by the teacher, takes the following form: I-R-P-R-P-R...E. The second version is an open chain of interaction, which is the same as the one above, but without the teacher's final evaluation.

Sharing ground, through making both information and reasoning explicit is the starting point for any type of authentic dialogue to take place. This sharing is usually manifested through freely exploring ideas and arguments, in a format of talk usually referred to as "exploratory talk" (ET). ET was proposed as "a way of using language effectively for joint, explicit, collaborative reasoning" (Mercer, Wegerif, & Dawes, 1999; p. 97). One of the main criteria for its distinction from the other two predominant types of classroom talk, namely accumulative and disputational talks, is that it embraces both critical and constructive engagement with each other's ideas (Mercer, 2004). Exploratory talk can either be initial, i.e., at an information-seeking level or more inquiry-related, for example when students are asked to explore variables in order to give answers to teacher-framed open questions. Examples of such questions are: 'What outcomes would you predict?' (in science) or 'Was decision x successful?' (in history). Students are invited to give *their own accounts* of why certain scientific phenomena take place, or why certain decisions were taken in a historical perspective, or what decision to take regarding a socio-scientific issue, for example.

---

[3] All these types of teacher's moves were initially proposed by Mercer (2000), but their proposal as versions of the Follow-up move is found in Lyle (2008).

One of the main distinctions between argumentation and other types of classroom talk is that the former includes three types of framing in a hierarchical and complementary way. These are: sensemaking, articulation, and persuasion (Berland & Reiser, 2009). When contextualized in an educational dialogue, each one of these may have at least two foci, as presented in Figure 6.1.

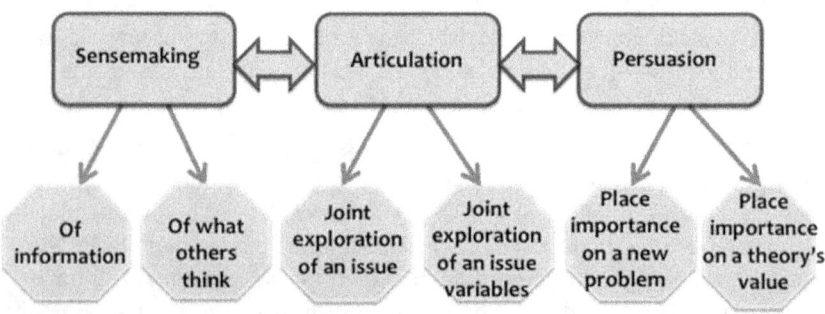

Figure 6.1. *Framing types in argumentative dialogue.*

What does this mean in practice?

Common intention

The first step from distinguishing between a dialogue, any type of dialogue, and a monologue is the manifestation of a shared intention. In the case of argumentation, this mainly corresponds to the need of the speakers of building common ground. If such a need is not made explicit by the speakers, usually the teachers, then we will most probably have a monologue rather than a dialogue. On the contrary, if the intention of building common ground is manifested by the participants, then a type of dialogue called information-seeking (see Chapter 3) is possible to emerge. The level of argumentativeness of this dialogue will then depend on how close the interaction chain is, based on what was said before regarding the variations of the IRE discourse pattern. Example 1, presented in Table 33, is a basic type of this dialogue with a close IRE pattern, whereas Example 2, presented in Table 34, is a more open sensemaking dialogue, in which the teacher replies with questions rather than giving the answers. Thus, a more sophisticated type of sensemaking is achieved.

Table 33. Dialogue example 1: Sensemaking through seeking the correct information (translated from Portuguese, History class, 8th grade).

Teacher	Let's start from where we left it last time, it was Brazil's discovery, wasn't it?
Bob	What page is it, teacher?
Teacher	We had seen the arrival in India. We finished the arrival at Calicut. Did we read everything? Ok, now let's summarise (.). How did the preparation of the overseas trip to India take place? The first trip, who was the [inaudible]?
choir	Ahh, Cristoforo Colombo.
Teacher	D. João II, isn't it? Pay attention, who was the one who started to prepare everything beforehand, first, he took care of what?
Marta	[inaudible] in the Atlantic
Teacher	In the Atlantic, no; in the Atlantic he knew how things were, didn't he? (.) It was in the Indian Ocean, wasn't it? He even sent the missionaries knowing about that, didn't he? What were their names? (.)Pêro of Covilhã and Afonso of Paiva, isn't it?
Teacher	In addition, he even took care of exploring which cost?
Charlie	The African.
Teacher	The occidental African coast. Through some important navigators, it was through whom?
Bob	Diogo Cão
Teacher	What did Diogo Cão explore?
Chris	The coast.
Teacher	The coast of what part of Africa?
Mary	Of Angola.
Teacher	Of Angola and of Namibia, isn't it? And after him, there was another navigator also sent by D. João II, who managed to make a big discovery, who was it?
choir	Bartolomeu Dias
Teacher	[The idea that] the Atlantic could communicate with the Indian, and this later leads to the preparation of the expedition of Vasco da Gama, as obviously who had already died?
choir	D. João II
Teacher	And who was his successor?
choir	D. Manuel.

Table 34. Dialogue example 2: Sensemaking through questioning (Biology, 7th grade, the excerpt is from an unpublished dataset in English).

James	..number 4 (the student invites the teacher to their group and asks about a particular question they are working on as a group).
Teacher	Right.
James	I'm thinking this [inaudible].
Teacher	Right. So why is it that we can't produce clones of ourselves?
James	Because we need science to do that.
Teacher	Yeah, but why can't we do it naturally? So plants...
James	Because it's got to be done chemically.
Teacher	...can produce clones. Yeah, but why, why? If we could just leave a plant,
James	Because we've got two parents.
Teacher	Right, so we have two parents. So why is it important that we have two parents?
James	So we have different characteristics.
Teacher	Yeah, you're right, that is true but why is it, that we can't have one parent? (goes through the book's pages as she talks) What do you need to produce a clone?
Chris	Two sex cells.
Teacher	(Nods No) What do you need asexually? So asexual reproduction is basically producing a clone, producing another plant.
Chris	Oh, that's nice.
James	Yeah, another dragon (students laugh).
Teacher	Why do you need Chris, why can plants reproduce asexually but we can't? What have they got that we haven't got? And it's in there.
James	Leaves? (students laugh).
Teacher	Right (looks in the book).
Chris	Pollen.
Teacher	OK, so as we grow we have lots of different types of cells and as we grow our cells become specialized.
James	They have specialized cells.
Teacher	OK, *we* have specialized cells, ok? Things that can reproduce asexually keep unspecialized cells. So they can use the unspecialized cells to produce a clone of themselves.
James	Oh, OK.
Teacher	We haven't got lots of unspecialized cells so we can't produce clones of ourselves.
James	Oh, alright.
Teacher	Is that alright? So that should answer 3 and 4 (moves to another students' group).

Knowledge construction

Articulating ideas through dialogue may take several forms. From a simple brainstorming or deep concept exploration, in which everyone's ideas are acknowledged, to an epistemic negotiation of concepts forming different explanations or solutions to a problem. A sense of inquiry is present in both types of articulation. However, what distinguishes argumentation from other inquiry-based types of dialogue is the need that this inquiry leads to some new knowledge, through co-constructive interactions between the teacher and the students or even among the students (although in whole class discussions this latter is more difficult to emerge, at least not to a high degree). The more argumentative the inquiry becomes, the deeper the knowledge constructed, or the other way around. Example 3, presented in Table 35, gives us a sense of what a beginning inquiry may look like, where young students explore a concept (house rules), presenting their ideas and contributing to each other through the teacher. Example 4, presented in Table 36, is a more advanced inquiry dialogue, in which students try to solve a problem exploring different variables.

Table 35. Dialogue example 3: Articulation through presenting ideas (translated from Portuguese, Civic education class, 7th grade).

Maria	Respect the space where we live (students brainstorm about values related to the concept of "home").
Teacher	Respect the space where we live. Who agrees with this rule by Maria, does everyone agree? Or no one?
Paul	Yes.
Teacher	This "yes" is nice! Why do you agree?
Paul	(.)
Peter	Because it is a nice rule.
Teacher	Because it is a nice rule… Say, Luke. What would you like to say in regards to this rule by Maria, what do you think?
Luke	I think it is correct. Because I hate it when my brothers come into my room and start to mess up.
Teacher	Do your brothers start doing what?
Luke	To disorganise it.
Teacher	To disorganize your space. So, respect the space of everyone. What do you all think? Respect the space of everyone. Ok… Do you all agree? Respect the space of everyone…
George	I don't know. I just have a room all by myself.

John	I don't.
Michael	Oh, I do have.
Teacher	So, when you don't have a room just for yourself…
Michael	We should respect the space of the others… Respect the other inhabitants (students laugh).
Luke	Respect the other residents.
Teacher	The other residents. But tell me something about this rule, respect everyone's space, does the space refer to a room?
Luke	Yes.
Peter	It could be.
Teacher	Let Luke say.
Luke	It could be the space that someone needs in order to reflect.
Teacher	Exactly, the space that everyone needs in order to reflect.
Luke	I share my room and I do have to do this, I live in…
Teacher	You share your room and you have to do this. And you, Michael, would you like to say anything?
Michael	No.
Teacher	No?
Choir	[inaudible] (Students speak at the same time).
Teacher	Respect the space of everyone. And now? Anything else you would like to say or is that all? Have a look at "home" (the word and concepts related to it from a previous brainstorm are written on the board). Have a look here: family, coziness, union, television, getting things off one's chest, love. Living together with family, eat, play, cook, sleep. And this serves us, after all, to think about the rules related to home, doesn't it? And the rules, what do they serve for? What do these rules serve for? Why do we write down these rules? Yes?

Table 36. Dialogue example 4: Articulation through negotiating solutions (Physics, 9th grade, the excerpt is from Scott et al., 2006, pp. 619-620).

Teacher	Now, what happens to the thermometer when its temperature goes up? What's happening in the thermometer? Does some kind of change take place?
Student 3	I think so, because the mercury in the thermometer only goes up and down, expands or contracts according to the temperature. It expands when the temperature is higher. It must have a heat change to go up and down.
Student 6	I think that the stuff in the thermometer is made of a material that doesn't take much heat to make it change. That's its property and that's why it's used in a thermometer. It's sensitive to whatever's being measured.

Some practical implications for argument-based teaching 99

Teacher	A good thermometer mustn't take too much heat otherwise it would lower the temperature of the object to be measured, OK?
Student 6	There is heat transfer, but the mercury doesn't take much. That's why it's used in thermometers, to measure the energy from the particles.
Teacher	There is a small amount of energy [transferred to the thermometer/mercury] but if there was no energy, would it be possible for the mercury to expand?
Student 7	No, I don't think it would.
Teacher	And there was an expansion of the mercury, wasn't there?
Student 8	Any change in heat, due to its sensitivity, changes its temperature. When you get this thermometer and put it in the surroundings, then it's at 25 °. When you put it in ice the temperature decreases so fast because the heat from the ice is higher and the mercury is sensitive to it and so it goes lower.
Student 6	And I think that the energy of the mercury will be equal to that of the ice that is moving faster and will make the mercury go up or down.
Teacher	Let's consider this situation you have mentioned. It was at 25°, and then you put it in the ice, and then the temperature decreased. And you are saying that the ice, in this situation, has more heat than the thermometer? Is there any heat transfer in this case? What is the direction of this heat change; heat transfer in this case?

Use of evidence

The use of evidence to persuade each other is an essential part of argumentation, as we already saw throughout this book. This persuasion is not always manifested as a pragmatic outcome (e.g., win a disagreement, revise one's own arguments, withdraw a position, etc.). At least in whole class teacher-guided dialogues persuasion is mainly manifested through the use of persuasive discourse, and the establishment of an implicit "rule" that for any argument to be valid, it is not enough to say "because I say so". This rule applies to both the teacher and the students. This simple affirmation has a series of implications for teaching and its transformation into a genuine interaction, in which authority is not established a priori, but it is embedded in the use of the right evidence and arguments. Deciding which problems, or aspects of a problem, students should look at most of the times is pre-defined by authorities, e.g. the teacher following the textbook. When the teacher allows that the problems arise from the students, or when (s)he places their attention to everyday familiar situations to which the curricular problems apply, a new type of dialogue resembling the discovery dialogue discussed in Chapter 3 is possible to be enacted. Table 37 presents an example of such a dialogue: after students were taught about the Portuguese discoveries and how the indigenous people were treated, the teacher drives the discussion towards the difference between assimilation and acculturation. Then students try to find examples from their everyday lives that best match one or another definition.

Table 37. Dialogue example 5 (translated from Portuguese, History, 8th grade).

Teacher	Ok, let's talk a little bit about that... what do you think about acculturation and assimilation? Do you think that, for example, when you get close, as Antonio said, to the American culture, you are doing what?
Antonio	Assimilating
Teacher	You're assimilating cultural data, aren't you? You're not doing any sort of acculturation (.).
Maria	We're not adopting that culture; we're not doing all their rituals.
Eugenia	We're not becoming ...
Maria	... Americans.
Eugenia	Exactly!
Teacher	Nowadays internet is a process of what?
Manuel	Cultural assimilation.
Teacher	Cultural assimilation, so when you have... so Leonor here will tell us in which moments she feels she's assimilating elements from another culture
Leonor	Ahh, when do I assimilate?
Teacher	Yes
Leonor	Hmmm, when I eat sushi?
Teacher	When you eat sushi, very well, food is a way of assimilation.
Carla	When I'm speaking another language.
Teacher	When you're speaking another language, very well.
Sofia	When we go to museums.
Teacher	Museums are already what type of culture? (.) very fixed.
Miguel	When we use the same customs, doing the same ... I don't know, using the same clothes.
Teacher	Very well. Now I'm not going to give out another big assimilation mechanism, which is what?
Manuel	Commerce.
Teacher	Hmm?
Manuel	Commerce.
Maria	Buying American goods.
Teacher	It's not just products.
Maria	The exportation, mister, the importation.
Teacher	[inaudible] They compete to see who has more ...?

Choir	More
Teacher	But you put there another word there
John	Concurrence?
Teacher	Brand, isn't it? There are also constant assimilation phenomena nowadays. Yes?
Carmen	When we enter the embassy.
Teacher	No, someone who enters an embassy, enters and leaves, is not assimilating anything.
Carmen	But it is as if we had entered another country.
Teacher	It's not another country, it's just another country formally.
Carmen	So when I go to America, do I assimilate the culture?
Teacher	When we travel we assimilate culture, it's true, but travelling is not the same thing as going to the embassy [] (everyone's speaking at the same time) But attention with globalization, it is not getting back to the initial concept, for example at this moment is there globalization?
John	No.
Manuel	Now, nowadays?
Teacher	No, in the era we were studying, XVI century.
Manuel	There's internationalization.
Many	It depends
Teacher	There's internationalization, it's possible to buy Chinese goods, it's possible to buy products from the Americas, but you need to live in big cities, that was for a minority of the population, less than 10%, imagine, because the majority, as I explained, the majority of the population was born, lived and died in a 5kms radius (.)
John	Only 5kms?
Teacher	That is, they didn't know, they didn't assimilate any culture, do you understand? And they didn't buy goods, they exchange them there in the village, the ones who are in touch with the whole world is different (.) this is [] already an assimilation, for example when the English went to live in India at the beginning they'd use oriental habits, a fashion called the orientalism was actually born. When you eat sushi now you're getting habits from the Orient, aren't you? But that's not acculturation (.) because what it is... you maintain your culture, you're just getting other aspects of the...
	Let's hear Antonio, John, do you want to be quiet in your chair?
Antonio	The immigrants...
Teacher	Very well, go on.
Antonio	Do they become part of the culture of the country they go to?
Teacher	But then there's also a mix, it's usually said that immigrants stick a little between two worlds.
Antonio	That's it.

Although the Dialogue example 5 above is more near to a persuasive dialogue, as students and teacher negotiate their ideas about whether a situation is more likely to be defined as acculturation or assimilation, it is still far from a purely dialectical interaction, in which viewpoints are openly negotiated, challenged, and potentially revised. The dialogue excerpt presented in Table 38 may be considered an example of a persuasion-oriented argumentation dialogue (another example was quoted in Chapter 3).

Table 38. Dialogue example 6 (translated from Portuguese, Natural sciences, 9th grade; the excerpt is from a whole class debate on whether or not we should do sports in the open air).

Andrew	Ok, the point is about the spaces ... in the closed spaces there is more transmission of bacteria and viruses between people ... so, everyone gets sick if someone gets sick. In the exterior, there are also bacteria and viruses, this is why we can also get sick. But... there is more oxygen than an interior space, because the air... is always the same, and when we inhale and exhale, it is ... there is more carbon dioxide getting out ... and therefore the concentration of carbon dioxide in the space starts to increase and that of oxygen to decrease...
Laura	One of the problems of doing sports in the open air is the solar exposition ... we have to carry ... if we are not protected, it can affect our skin, even when the sol is not ... even when it is cloudy ... [inaudible] (she goes on her reasoning mentioning also vitamin D)
Teacher	And how is it that vitamin D relates to that? Explain!
Laura	When ... if we are doing sports in the open air ... but being protected ... we can capture the sun's energy but not the vitamin D...
Teacher	When we are wearing sun protection, can we absorb vitamin D?
Choir	Yes!
Teacher	Do you agree with her?
Choir	Noooo!
Teacher	So, how is it?
Laura	...I may be mistaken, but when the vitamin D, it only gets absorbed, if we have...if we don't wear sun protection ... []
Teacher	It is not about being protected or not protected. It is ... when the sun... it projects on our skin, doesn't it? There is a substance, let's say, in our skin, called pro-vitamin D and the sun helps this substance to be transformed into vitamin D ... and so, go on with your reasoning... how is it now?
James	Miss, but how is it that ... if we put on sun protection, we don't captivate any vitamin D? If not, then it is bad to wear any protection ... shall I put the protection or take in vitamin D? It doesn't sound good, we have to have our sun protection on ... (students laugh)

Teacher	So? How can we solve this?
Choir	[inaudible] (students talk simultaneously)
Andrew	We can be outdoors during the hours that it is not as hot ... that is ... we cannot be in the sun between 10 in the morning and 4 in the afternoon.

To summarize, argumentation as a dialogic practice allows for joint action to become shared, co-intention to be manifested as knowledge construction, and epistemic agency to be expressed as a negotiation of the quality and strength of the arguments put forward. These sub-goals may be expressed at any point of interaction in the form of dialogic sequences. All of them serve the upper goal of dialogue-based pedagogy, which is the promotion of a critical thinking attitude and the transformation of the classroom into an epistemic community of inquiry.

One of the main limitations of the approach adopted here refers to the fact that it only focuses on the epistemic aspects of argumentation as a type of pedagogical dialogue. Recent research places increased attention on the role of emotions in the development and effect of argumentative discussions both in the classroom and in computer-supported collaborative learning environment (e.g., Polo, Lund, Plantin, & Niccolai 2016). The strong connection between argumentation and emotions, as manifested in discourse, opens up new paths for dialogue and education research.

References

Abi-El-Mona, I., & Abd-El-Khalick, F. (2006). Argumentative discourse in a high school chemistry classroom. *School Science and Mathematics, 106*(8), 349-361. Doi: 10.1111/j.1949-8594.2006.tb17755.x

Aguiar, O., Mortimer, E. F., & Scott, P. (2010). Learning from and responding to students' questions: The authoritative and dialogic tension. Journal of Research in Science Teaching, 47(2), 174–193.

Alexander, R. (2008*). Essays of pedagogy.* London, UK: Routledge.

Asterhan, C. S., & Schwarz, B. B. (2016). Argumentation for learning: Well-trodden paths and unexplored territories. *Educational Psychologist, 51*(2), 164-187.

Atwood, S., Turnbull, W., & Carpendale, J. I. M. (2010). The Construction of Knowledge in Classroom Talk. The Journal of the Learning Sciences, 19(3), 358–402. https://doi.org/10.1080/10508406201048101

Avraamidou, L., & Zembal-Saul, C. (2005). Giving priority to evidence in science teaching: A first-year elementary teacher's specialized practices and knowledge. *Journal of Research in Science Teaching, 42*(9), 965-986. Doi:10.1002/tea.20081

Baker, M. (2003). Computer-mediated argumentative interactions for the co-elaboration of scientific notions. In J. Andriessen, M. Baker, & D. Suthers (Eds.), *Arguing to learn. Confronting cognitions in computer-supported collaborative learning environments* (pp. 47–78). Amsterdam: Springer.

Baron, J. (1995). Myside bias in thinking about abortion. Thinking and Reasoning, 1, 221–235.

Barth, E. M., & Krabbe, E. C. (1982). *From axiom to dialogue: A philosophical study of logics and argumentation.* Berlin, Germany: Walter de Gruyter.

Bell, P. & Linn, M.C. (2000). Scientific arguments as learning artifacts : designing for learning from the web with KIE. *International Journal of Science Education, 22*(8), 797-817. Doi:10.1080/095006900412284

Berland, L. K., & Hammer, D. (2012). Framing for scientific argumentation. *Journal of Research in Science Teaching, 49*(1), 68-94. Doi:10.1002/tea.20446

Berland, L. K., & McNeill, K. L. (2010). A learning progression for scientific argumentation: Understanding student work and supportive instructional contexts. *Science Education, 94*(5), 765-793. Doi:10.1002/sce.20402

Berland, L. K., & Reiser, B. J. (2009). Making sense of argumentation and explanation. *Science Education, 93*(1), 26–55. Doi:10.1002/sce.20286

Berland, L. K., & Reiser, B. J. (2011). Classroom communities' adaptations of the practice of scientific argumentation. *Science Education, 95*(2), 191-216.

Bransford, J.D., Brown A.L., & Cocking, R.R. (2000) (Eds.). How people learn: Brain, mind, experience and school. Washington, DC: National Academy Press.

Braund, M., Scholtz, Z., Sadeck, M., & Koopman, R. (2013). First steps in teaching argumentation: A South African study. *International Journal of Educational Development, 33*(2), 175-184. Doi: 10.1016/j.ijedudev.2012.03.007

Brem, S. K. & Rips, L. J. (2000). Explanation and evidence in informal argument. *Cognitive Science, 24*, 573-604.

Brough, C. J. (2012). Implementing the democratic principles and practices of student-centred curriculum integration in primary schools. *Curriculum Journal, 23*(3), 345-369.

Bulgren, J. A., Ellis, J. D., & Marquis, J. G. (2014). The use and effectiveness of an argumentation and evaluation intervention in science classes. *Journal of Science Education and Technology, 23*(1), 82-97.

Cavagnetto, A. R. (2010). Argument to foster scientific literacy: A review of argument interventions in K–12 science contexts. *Review of Educational Research, 80*(3), 336-371.

Chen, Y.-Ch., Hand, B., & Norton-Meier, L. (2016). Teacher roles of questioning in early elementary science classrooms: A framework promoting student cognitive complexities in argumentation. *Research in Science Education* [Online first]. Doi: 10.1007/s11165-015-9506-6

Chin, C., Osborne, J. (2010). Students' questions and discursive interaction: Their impact on argumentation during collaborative group discussions in science. *Journal of Research in Science Teaching, 47*(7), 883-908. Doi:10.1002/tea.20385

Chin, C., & Teou, L. Y. (2009). Using concept cartoons in formative assessment: Scaffolding students' argumentation. *International Journal of Science Education, 31*(10), 1307-1332.

Chinn, C. A. (2011). Learning to argue. In O´Donnell, A. O., Hmelo-Silver, C. E., & Erkens, G. (Eds.), *Collaborative learning, reasoning, and technology* (pp. 355-385). New York: Routledge.

Chinn, C. A., & Brewer, W. F. (1998). An empirical test of a taxonomy of responses to anomalous data in science. *Journal of Research in Science teaching, 35*(6), 623-654.

Choi, A., Klein, V., & Hershberger, S. (2015). Success, difficulty, and instructional strategy to enact an argument-based inquiry approach: experiences of elementary teachers. *International Journal of Science and Mathematics Education, 13*(5), 991-1011. Doi: 10.1007/s10763-014-9525-1

Dawson, V. M., & Venville, G. (2010). Teaching strategies for developing students' argumentation skills about socioscientific issues in high school genetics. *Research in Science Education, 40*, 133-148. Doi: 10.1007/s11165-008-9104-y

De La Paz, S., Ferretti, R., Wissinger, D., Yee, L., & MacArthur, C. (2012). Adolescents' disciplinary use of evidence, argumentative strategies, and organizational structure in writing about historical controversies. *Written Communication, 29*(4), 412-454.

Dicks, D., & Ives, C. (2008). Instructional designers at work: A study of how designers design. *Canadian Journal of Learning and Technology/La revue canadienne de l'apprentissage et de la technologie, 34*(2).

Driver, R., Newton, P., & Osborne, J. (2000). Establishing the norms of scientific argumentation in classrooms. *Science Education, 84*(3), 287-312. Doi: 10.1002/(SICI)1098-237X(200005)84:3<287::AID-SCE1>3.3.CO;2-1

Duschl, R. A., & Osborne, J. (2002). Supporting and promoting argumentation discourse in science education. *Studies in Science Education, 38*, 39-72. Doi:10.1080/03057260208560187

Ellsworth, E. (1989). Why doesn't this feel empowering? Working through the repressive myths of critical pedagogy. *Harvard educational review, 59*(3), 297-325.

Elo, S. & Kyngäs, H. (2008). The qualitative content analysis process. *Journal of Advanced Nursing, 62*(1), 107-115.

Erduran, S., Simon, S., & Osborne, J. (2004). TAPping into argumentation: Developments in the application of Toulmin's Argument Pattern for studying science discourse. *Science Education, 88*(6), 915–933. Doi: 10.1002/sce.20012

EU (2006). Recommendation of the European Parliament and of the Council of 18 December 2006 on key competences for lifelong learning. Official Journal of the European Union, Brussels, Belgium.

Evagorou, M., & Dillon, J. (2011). Argumentation in the teaching of science. In Corrigan, D. et al. (Eds), *The professional knowledge base of science teaching* (pp. 189-203). Netherlands: Springer.

Felton, M. (2004). The development of discourse strategies in adolescent argumentation. *Cognitive Development, 19*(1), 35–52.

Felton, M., Garcia-Mila, M., Villarroel, C., & Gilabert, S. (2015). Arguing collaboratively: Argumentative discourse types and their potential for knowledge building. *British Journal of Educational Psychology, 85*(3), 372-386. Doi:10.1111/bjep.12078

Filatro, A., & Piconez, S. C. B. (2004). *Design instrucional contextualizado*. São Paulo: Senac.

Ford, M. (2008). Disciplinary authority and accountability in scientific practice and learning. *Science Education, 92*(3), 404-423. Doi: 10.1002/sce.20263

Freeman, J. B. (2006). Systematizing Toulmin's warrants: an epistemic approach. In Proceedings of The Uses of Argument Conference, McMaster University, 18-21 May 2005. Available at: https://tinyurl.com/ycxhof47

Glassner, A., & Schwarz, B. (2007). What stands and develops between creative and critical thinking? Argumentation? *Thinking Skills & Creativity, 2*(1), 10–18.

Gordon, T. F., Prakken, H., & Walton, D. (2007). The Carneades model of argument and burden of proof. *Artificial Intelligence, 171*(10-15), 875-896.

Govier, T. (2014). *A practical study of argument* (7th edition). Boston: Wadsworth & Cengage Learning.

Graff, G. (2003). *Clueless in academe* (Vol. 2). New Haven, CT: Yale University Press.

Harrison, C., & Howard, S. (2009). *Inside the primary black box: Assessment for learning in primary and early years classrooms*. Brentford, UK: Granada Learning Assessment.

Hennessey, M. G. (2003). Probing the dimensions of metacognition: Implications for conceptual change teaching-learning. In G. M. Sinatra and P. R. Pintrich (Eds.), *Intentional conceptual change* (pp. 103-132). Mahwah, NJ: Lawrence Erlbaum Associates.

Herrenkohl, L. R., & Cornelius, L. (2013) Investigating elementary students' scientific and historical argumentation. *Journal of the Learning Sciences, 22*(3), 413-461. Doi: 10.1080/10508406.2013.799475

Herrenkohl, L.R., Palinscar, A. S., DeWater, L.S., & Kawasaki, K. (1999). Developing scientific communities in classrooms: A socio-cognitive approach. *The Journal of the Learning Sciences, 8*(3&4), 451-493.

Hmelo-Silver, C. E. (2011). Design principles for scaffolding technology-based inquiry. In O´Donnell, A. O., Hmelo-Silver, C. E., & Erkens, G. (Eds.), *Collaborative learning, reasoning, and technology* (pp. 147-170). New York: Routledge.

Hogan, P., & Smith, R. (2003). The activity of philosophy and the practice of education. In Blake, N., Smeyers, P., Smith, R., & Standish, P. (Eds.), *The Blackwell guide to the philosophy of education* (pp. 165-180). Oxford, UK: Blackwell Publishing.

Hopkins, N. (2014). The democratic curriculum: Concept and Practice. *Journal of Philosophy of Education, 48*(3), 416-427.

Hundal, S., Levin, D. M., & Keselman, A. (2014). Lessons of researcher-teacher co-design of an environmental health afterschool club curriculum. *International Journal of Science Education, 36*(9), 1510-1530. Doi: 10.1080/09500693.2013.844377

Hutchison, P., & Hammer, D. (2010). Attending to student epistemological framing in a science classroom. *Science Education, 94*(3), 506-524. Doi: 10.1002/sce.20373

Jiménez-Aleixandre, M. P., Rodriguez, A. B., & Duschl, R. A. (2000). "Doing the lesson" or "doing science": Argument in high school genetics. *Science Education, 84*(6), 757-792. Doi: 10.1002/1098-237X(200011)84:6<757::AID-SCE5>3.0.CO;2-F

Johnson, R. H. (1996). *The rise of Informal logic*. Newport: Vale Press.

Kelly, G. J., Druker, S., & Chen, C. (1998). Students' reasoning about electricity: combining performance assessments with argumentation analysis. *International Journal of Science Education, 20*(7), 849-871.

Kennedy, N., & Kennedy, D. (2011). Community of philosophical inquiry as a discursive structure, and its role in school curriculum design. *Journal of Philosophy of Education, 45*(2), 265-283.

Knight-Bardsley, A., & McNeill, K. L. (2016). Teachers' pedagogical design capacity for scientific argumentation. *Science Education, 100*(4), 645-672. Doi: 10.1002/sce.21222

Kreijns, K., Kirschner, P. A., & Jochems, W. (2003). Identifying the pitfalls for social interaction in computer-supported collaborative learning environments: a review of the research. *Computers in human behavior, 19*(3), 335-353.

Kuhn, D. (1991). *The skills of argument*. Cambridge: Cambridge University Press.

Kuhn, D. (1992). Thinking as argument. *Harvard Educational Review, 62*, 155-179.

Kuhn, D. (2001). How do people know?. *Psychological science, 12*(1), 1-8.

Kuhn, D., & Crowell, A. (2011). Dialogic argumentation as a vehicle for developing young adolescents' thinking. *Psychological Science, 22*(4), 545-552.

Kuhn, D., & Park, S. H. (2005). Epistemological understanding and the development of intellectual values. *International Journal of Educational Research, 43*(3), 111-124.

Kuhn, D., & Udell, W. (2003). The development of argument skills. *Child Development, 74*(5), 1245-1260.

Kuhn, D., Shaw, V., & Felton, M. (1997). Effects of dyadic interaction on argumentative reasoning. *Cognition and instruction, 15*(3), 287-315.

Kuhn, T. S. (1970) (2nd edition). *The structure of scientific revolutions.* Chicago, IL: University of Chicago Press.

Lampert, M. (1986). Knowing, doing, and teaching multiplication. *Cognition and instruction, 3*(4), 305-342.

Larrain, A., Freire, P., & Howe, C. (2014). Science teaching and argumentation : One-sided versus dialectical argumentation in Chilean middle-school science lessons. *International Journal of Science Education, 36*(6), 1017-1036. Doi: 10.1080/09500693.2013.832005

Latour, B. (1987). *Science in action: How to follow scientists and engineers through society.* Cambridge, MA: Harvard University Press.

Lehrer, R., & Schauble, L. (2005). Developing modeling and argument in elementary grades. In T. A. Romberg, T. P. Carpenter, & F. Dremock (Eds.), *Understanding mathematics and science matters* (pp. 29–53). Mahwah, NJ: Lawrence Erlbaum.

Leigh, F. (2007). Platonic dialogue, maieutic method and critical thinking. *Journal of Philosophy of Education, 41*(3), 309-323.

Leitão, S. (2000). The potential of argument in knowledge building. *Human development, 43*(6), 332-360.

Lemke, J. (1990). *Talking science: Language, learning, and values.* Norwood, NJ: Ablex.

Lin, S. S., & Mintzes, J. J. (2010). Learning argumentation skills through instruction in socioscientific issues: The effect of ability level. *International Journal of Science and Mathematics Education, 8*(6), 993-1017.

Litman, C., & Greenleaf, C. (2017). Argumentation tasks in secondary English language arts, history, and science: Variations in instructional focus and inquiry space. *Reading Research Quarterly* [online first].

Louca, L. T., Zacharia, Z. C., & Tzialli, D. (2012). Identification, Interpretation-Evaluation, Response: An alternative framework for analyzing teacher discourse in science. *International Journal of Science Education, 34*(12), 1823-1856. Doi: 10.1080/09500693.2012.671971

Lund, K., Molinari, G., Séjourné, A., & Baker, M. (2007). How do argumentation diagrams compare when student pairs use them as a means for debate or as a tool for representing debate ? *Computer-Supported Collaborative Learning, 2*(2-3), 273–295. Doi: 10.1007/s11412-007-9019-z

Lyle, S. (2008). Dialogic teaching: Discussing theoretical contexts and reviewing evidence from classroom practice. *Language and Education, 22*(3), 222–240.

Macagno, F. (2016). Argument relevance and structure. Assessing and developing students' uses of evidence. *International Journal of Educational Research, 79*, 180-194.

Macagno, F., Mayweg-Paus, E., & Kuhn, D. (2015). Argumentation theory in education studies: Coding and improving students' argumentative strategies. *Topoi, 34*(2), 523-537.

Manz, E. (2015). Representing student argumentation as functionally emergent from scientific activity. *Review of Educational Research, 85*(4), 553-590.

Martin, A. M., & Hand, B. (2009). Factors affecting the implementation of argument in the elementary science classroom. A longitudinal case study. *Research in Science Education, 39*(1), 17-38. Doi:10.1007/s11165-007-9072-7

Matthews, G. B. (1999). *Socratic perplexity and the nature of Philosophy.* Oxford: Oxford University Press.

Mayes, G. R. (2010). Argument explanation complementarity and the structure of informal reasoning. *Informal Logic, 30*(1), 92-111.

McDonald, C. V. (2010). The influence of explicit nature of science and argumentation instruction on preservice primary teachers' views of nature of science. *Journal of Research in Science Teaching, 47*(9), 1137-1164. Doi: 10.1002/tea.20377

McNeill, K. L. (2009). Teachers' use of curriculum to support students in writing scientific arguments to explain phenomena. *Science Education, 93*(2), 233-268. Doi: 10.1002/sce.20294

McNeill, K. L. (2011). Elementary students' views of explanation, argumentation, and evidence, and their abilities to construct arguments over the school year. *Journal of Research in Science Teaching, 48*(7), 793-823. Doi: 10.1002/tea.20430

McNeill, K. L., & Knight, A. M. (2013). Teachers' pedagogical content knowledge of scientific argumentation : The impact of professional development on K–12 teachers. *Science Education, 97*(6), 936-972. Doi: 10.1002/sce.21081

McNeill, K. L., & Krajcik, J. (2008). Scientific explanations: Characterizing and evaluating the effects of teachers' instructional practices on student learning. *Journal of Research in Science Teaching, 45*(1), 53-78. Doi: 10.1002/tea.20201

McNeill, K. L., & Pimentel, D. S. (2010). Scientific discourse in three urban classrooms: The role of the teacher in engaging high school students in argumentation. *Science Education, 94*(2), 203-229. Doi: 10.1002/sce.20364

McNeill, K. L., González-Howard, M., Katsh-Singer, R., & Loper, S. (2016). Pedagogical content knowledge of argumentation: Using classroom contexts to assess high-quality PCK rather than pseudoargumentation. *Journal of Research in Science Teaching, 53*(2), 261-290. Doi: 10.1002/tea.21252

McNeill, K. L., Lizotte, D. J., Krajcik, J., & Marx, R. W. (2006). Supporting students' construction of scientific explanations by fading scaffolds in instructional materials. *The Journal of the Learning Sciences, 15*(2), 153-191.

McNeill, K. L., Pimentel, D. S., & Strauss, E. G. (2013). The impact of high school science teachers' beliefs, curricular enactments and experience on student learning during an inquiry-based urban ecology curriculum. *International Journal of Science Education, 35*(15), 2608-2644. Doi: 10.1080/09500693.2011.618193

Mehan, H. (1979). 'What time is it, Denise?": Asking known information questions in classroom discourse. *Theory into practice, 18*(4), 285-294.

Mercer, N. (2004). Sociocultural discourse analysis. *Journal of Applied Linguistics, 1*(2), 137–168.

Mercer, N., Dawes, L., & Staarman, J. K. (2009). Dialogic teaching in the primary science classroom. *Language and Education, 23*(4), 353-369.

Mercer, N., Wegerif, R., & Dawes, L. (1999). Children's talk and the development of reasoning in the classroom. *British Educational Research Journal, 25*(1), 95–111.

Mercier, H. (2011). Reasoning serves argumentation in children. *Cognitive Development, 26*(3), 177-191.

Mitchell, S., & Andrews, R. (eds) (2000). *Learning to argue in Higher Education*. Heinemann.

Mortimer, E., & Scott, P. (2003). *Meaning making in secondary science classrooms*. McGraw-Hill Education.

Newton, P., Driver, R., & Osborne, J. (1999). The place of argumentation in the pedagogy of school science. *International Journal of Science Education, 21*(5), 553-576.

NRC (1996). *National Science Education Standards*. Washington, DC: National Academy Press.

NRC (2007). *Taking science to school: Learning and teaching science in grades K-8*. Washington, DC: National Academy Press.

Nussbaum, E. M., Sinatra, G., & Poliquin, A. (2008). Role of epistemic beliefs and scientific argumentation in science learning. *International Journal of Science Education, 30*, 1977-1999.

Nussbaum, E. M. (2011). Argumentation, dialogue theory, and probability modeling: Alternative frameworks for argumentation research in education. *Educational Psychologist, 46*(2), 84-106.

Nussbaum, E. M. & Sinatra, G. M. (2003). Argument and conceptual engagement. *Contemporary Educational Psychology, 28*, 573-595.

Osborne, A. (2005). Debate and student development in the history classroom. *New Directions for Teaching and Learning, 103*, 39-50.

Osborne, J. (2010). Arguing to learn in science: The role of collaborative, critical discourse. *Science, 328*(5977), 463-466.

Osborne, J., Erduran, S., & Simon, S. (2004). Enhancing the quality of argumentation in school science. *Journal of Research in Science Teaching, 41*, 994–1020. Doi: 10.1002/tea.20035

Osborne, J. F., & Patterson, A. (2011). Scientific argument and explanation: A necessary distinction?. *Science Education, 95*(4), 627-638.

Papastephanou, M., & Angeli, C. (2007). Critical thinking beyond skill. *Educational Philosophy and Theory, 39*(6), 604-621.

Peirce Ch. S. (1878). How to make our ideas clear. In N. Houser & Ch. Kloesel (Eds), *The essential Peirce*, Volume 1. Bloomington: Indiana University Press.

Perkins, D. N., Farady, M., & Bushey, B. (1991). Everyday reasoning and the roots of intelligence. In *Informal Reasoning and Education* (pp. 83–105). Mahwah: Lawrence Erlbaum Associates.

Politis, V. (2006). Aporia and searching in early Plato. In Judson, L. & V. Karasmanēs (eds.), *Remembering Socrates: Philosophical Essays* (pp. 87-109). Oxford, UK: Oxford University Press.

Politis, V. (2015). The structure of enquiry in Plato's early dialogues. Cambridge, UK: Cambridge University Press.

Polo, C., Lund, K., Plantin, C., & Niccolai, G. P. (2016). Group emotions: The social and cognitive functions of emotions. International Journal of Computer-Supported Collaborative Learning, 11(2), 123–156.

Psillos St. (2011). An explorer upon untrodden ground: Peirce on abduction. In D. Gabbay, St. Hartmann, & J. Woods (Eds.), *Handbook of the history of logic*, (pp. 117–151). Oxford: NorthHolland.

Rapanta, C. (2018). Teaching as abductive reasoning: The role of argumentation. *Informal Logic, 38*(2), 293-311.

Rapanta, C., Garcia-Mila, M., & Gilabert, S. (2013). What is meant by argumentative competence? An integrative review of methods of analysis and assessment in education. *Review of Educational Research, 83*(4), 483-520.

Reznitskaya, A., & Wilkinson, I. (2017). *The most reasonable answer: Helping students build better arguments together*. Cambridge, MA: Harvard Education Press.

Reznitskaya, A., Anderson, R., McNurlen, B., Nguyen-Jahiel, K., Archoudidou, A., & Kim, S. (2001). Influence of oral discussion on written argument. *Discourse Processes, 32*, 155-175.

Reznitskaya, A., Wilkinson, I., Oyler, J., Bourdage, K., & Sykes, A. (2016). Using the Argumentation Rating Tool to support teacher facilitation of inquiry dialogue in elementary Language Arts classrooms. Paper presented at the Annual Meeting of the American Educational Research Association, Washington, DC.

Risen, J., & Gilovich, T. (2007). Informal logical fallacies. In R. J. Sternberg, H. L. Roediger, & D. F. Halpern (Eds.), Critical thinking in Psychology (pp. 110–130). New York: Cambridge University Press.

Romiszowski, A. J. (2004). *Designing instructional systems: Decision making in course planning and curriculum design*. London: Routledge Falmer.

Roschelle, J., & Teasley, S. D. (1995). The construction of shared knowledge in collaborative problem solving. In C. O´Malley (Ed.), *Computer supported collaborative learning* (pp. 69–97). Berlin: Springer.

Russ, R. S., Coffey, J. E., Hammer, D., & Hutchison, P. (2009). Making classroom assessment more accountable to scientific reasoning: A case for attending to mechanistic thinking. *Science Education, 93*, 875-891. Doi: 10.1002/sce.20320

Sadler, T. D. (2006). Promoting discourse and argumentation in science teacher education. *Journal of Science Teacher Education, 17*, 323-346. Doi: 10.1007/s10972-006-9025-4

Sadler, T. D., & Fowler, S. R. (2006). A threshold model of content knowledge transfer for socioscientific argumentation. *Science education, 90*, 986-1004. doi: 10.1002/sce.20165

Sampson, V., & Blanchard, M. R. (2012). Science teachers and scientific argumentation: Trends in views and practice. *Journal of Research in Science Teaching, 49*(9), 1122-1148. Doi: 10.1002/tea.21037

Sampson, V., & Clark, D. B. (2008). Assessment of the ways students generate arguments in science education: Current perspectives and recommendations for future directions. *Science Education, 92*(3), 447-472. Doi: 10.1002/sce.20276

Sandoval, W. A. (2003). Conceptual and epistemic aspects of students' scientific explanations. *Journal of the Learning Sciences, 12*(1), 5-51.

Sandoval, W. A. (2005). Understanding students' practical epistemologies and their influence on learning through inquiry. *Science Education, 89*(4), 634-656.

Sandoval, W. A., & Millwood, K. A. (2005). The quality of students' use of evidence in written scientific explanations. *Cognition and Instruction, 23*(1), 23–55.

Schmit, J. S. (2002). Different questions, bigger answers: Matching the scope of inquiry to students' needs. In Holden, J., & Schmit, J. S. (Eds). *Inquiry and the Literary Text: Constructing Discussions in the English Classroom. Classroom Practices in Teaching English*. Urbana, USA: National Council of Teachers of English.

Schoerning, E., Hand, B., Shelley, M., & Therrien, W. (2015). Language, access, and power in the elementary science classroom. *Science Education, 99*(2), 238-259. Doi: 10.1002/sce.21154

Schwarz, B. B., & Baker, M. J. (2016). *Dialogue, argumentation and education: History, theory and practice*. New York: Cambridge University Press.

Schwarz, B. B., & Shahar, N. (2017). Combining the dialogic and the dialectic: Putting argumentation into practice in classroom talk. *Learning, Culture and Social Interaction, 12*, 113-132.

Schwarz, B. B., Neuman, Y., Gil, J., & Ilya, M. (2003). Construction of collective and individual knowledge in argumentative activity. *Journal of the Learning Sciences, 12*(2), 219-256.

Scott, P. H., Mortimer, E. F., & Aguiar, O. G. (2006). The tension between authoritative and dialogic discourse: A fundamental characteristic of meaning making interactions in high school science lessons. *Science Education, 90*(4), 605-631. Doi: 10.1002/sce.20131

Sedova, K., Sedlacek, M., & Svaricek, R. (2016). Teacher professional development as a means of transforming student classroom talk. *Teaching and Teacher Education, 57*, 14-25.

Shemwell, J. T., Gwarjanski, K. R., Capps, D. K., Avargil, S., & Meyer, J. L. (2015). Supporting teachers to attend to generalization in science classroom argumentation. *International Journal of Science Education, 37*(4), 599-628. Doi: 10.1080/09500693.2014.1000428

Shulman, L. (1987). Knowledge and teaching: Foundations of the new reform. *Harvard educational review, 57*(1), 1-23.

Simon, S. (2008). Using Toulmin's argument pattern in the evaluation of argumentation in school science. *International Journal of Research & Method in Education, 31*(3), 277-289.

Simon, S., Erduran, S., & Osborne, J. (2006). Learning to teach argumentation: Research and development in the science classroom. *International Journal of Science Education, 28*(2-3), 235-260. Doi: 10.1080/09500690500336957

Smith, R. (2014). Re-reading Plato: the slow cure for knowledge. In Papastephanou, M., Strand, T., & Pirrie, A. (Eds.), *Philosophy as a lived experience: Navigating the dichotomies between thought and action* (pp. 23-37). Berlin: LIT Verlag.

Toulmin, S. (1958). *The uses of argument.* Cambridge, UK: Cambridge University Press.

Toulmin, S., Rieke, R., & Janik, A. (1984). *An introduction to reasoning* (2nd edition). New York: Mcmillan.

van Gelder, T., Bissett, M., & Cumming, G. (2004). Cultivating expertise in informal reasoning. *Canadian Journal of Experimental Psychology, 58*(2), 142-152.

Van Lier, L. (1994). Language awareness, contingency and interaction. *AILA Review, 11*, 69-82.

Varelas, M., Pappas, C. C., Kane, J. M., Arsenault, A., Hankes, J., & Cowan, B. M. (2008). Urban primary-grade children think and talk science: Curricular and instructional practices that nurture participation and argumentation. *Science Education, 92*(1), 65-95. Doi: 10.1002/sce.20232

Von Aufschaiter, C., Erduran, S., Osborne, J., & Simon, S. (2008). Arguing to learn and learning to argue: case studies on how students' argumentation relates to their scientific knowledge. *Journal of Research in Science Teaching, 45*(1), 101-131. Doi: 10.1002/tea.20213

Voss, J. F. (2005). Toulmin's model and the solving of ill-structured problems. *Argumentation, 19*, 321-329.

Walton, D. (2001). Abductive, presumptive and plausible arguments. *Informal Logic, 21*(2).

Walton, D. N. (1989). Dialogue theory for critical thinking. *Argumentation, 3*, 169-184. Doi: 10.1007/BF00128147

Walton, D. N. (1996). *Argumentation schemes for presumptive reasoning.* Mahwah, NJ: Lawrence Erlbaum Associates.

Walton, D. N. (1998). *The new dialectic.* Toronto: University of Toronto Press.

Walton, D. N. (2005). *Abductive reasoning.* Tuscaloosa: University of Alabama Press.

Walton, D. N. (2008). *Informal logic: A pragmatic approach* (2nd Edition). Cambridge: Cambridge University Press.

Walton, D. N. (2011). An argumentative model of deliberative decision-making. In J. Yearwood, & A. Stranieri (Eds.), *Technologies for Supporting Reasoning Communities: Cooperative Approaches* (pp. 1-17). Ballarat: IGI Global.

Walton, D. N., Reed, C., & Macagno, F. (2008). *Argumentation schemes.* Cambridge: Cambridge University Press.

Walton, D., & Krabbe, E. (1995). *Commitment in dialogue*. Albany: State University of New York Press.

Wang, H. (2005). Aporias, responsibility, and the im/possibility of teaching multicultural education. *Educational Theory, 55*(1), 45-59.

Wegerif, R. (2008). Dialogic or dialectic? The significance of ontological assumptions in research on educational dialogue. *British Educational Research Journal, 34*(3), 347-361.

Weinberger, A., & Fischer, F. (2006). A framework to analyse argumentative knowledge construction in computer-supported collaborative learning. *Computers & Education, 46*(1), 71-95.

Wells, G. (1993). Reevaluating the IRF sequence: A proposal for the articulation of theories of activity and discourse for the analysis of teaching and learning in the classroom. *Linguistics and education, 5*(1), 1-37.

Wilkinson, I. A. G., Reznitskaya, A., Bourdage, K., Oyler, J., Glina, M., Drewry, R., ... Nelson, K. (2017). Toward a more dialogic pedagogy: changing teachers' beliefs and practices through professional development in language arts classrooms. *Language and education, 31*(1, SI), 65–82. Doi: 10.1080/09500782.2016.1230129

Wolfe, C. R., & Britt, M. A. (2008). The locus of the myside bias in written argumentation. *Thinking & Reasoning, 14*(1), 1-27.

Yang, Y. T. C., Newby, T. J., & Bill, R. L. (2005). Using Socratic questioning to promote critical thinking skills through asynchronous discussion forums in distance learning environments. *The American Journal of Distance Education, 19*(3), 163-181.

Yun, S. M., & Kim, H.-B. (2014). Changes in students´ participation and small group norms in scientific argumentation. *Research in Science Education, 45*(3), 465-484. Doi: 10.1007/s11165-014-9432-z

Zohar, A., & Nemet, F. (2002). Fostering students' knowledge and argumentation skills through dilemmas in human genetics. *Journal of Research in Science Teaching, 39*, 35–62. Doi: 10.1002/tea.10008

Appendix

Argument-based activity in Civic education

Context

Portuguese 7th grade (age 12-13 years old) Civic Education class. The curricular program is concentrated on civic values and duties, and it is quite flexible to include any type of activities that can help young adolescents understand the main components of civic life, education, and society.

Focus

The focus of the activity is on "Family" and what family means in different contexts and situations.

Structure of the activity

The activity was structured in four 90-minute sessions (this was possible given the flexibility of the curricular program). Each session was structured as follows:

Session 1 (90 minutes). The class started with a trigger: a powerpoint presentation with images and phrases related to the topic of "Family". The images were found online by the teacher and represented types of families, situations that families face (e.g. image of a refugees' family), and feelings related to being in/with one's family. The phrases chosen as stimuli were the following (translated from Portuguese): "It is only because of her that I don't feel being in a desert" (by José Saramago), "(...) bigger than humanity" (by Mia Couto), "What is family if not the most admirable of all governments?" (by Henri Lacordaire), "It is my home" (by José Luís Peixoto). Three of the four authors are very well-known in Portugal.

After this triggering activity, students sat in their groups (5-6 students per group), and they had to go through the following four activities: a) group administration regarding the choice of family roles that each one of the group members would play (e.g. father, mother, daughter, son, grandfather, etc.), the choice of a group moderator, the choice of a spokesperson, the choice of a secretary (who would write down everything said and decided within the group), and the creation of a name for the family represented by the group; b) individual reflection activity consisting of choosing one question of the ones appearing on Figure A.1 and write a reply justifying the answer following the template presented on Figure A.2; c) group reflection and debate, after reading three small texts in Portuguese (two poems and one excerpt of a leader's discourse) treating the topic of "Family" from different angles; d) redaction of a group response following the template presented on Figure A.3; e) presentation to the class of the written group reply to the initial question-issue "What is a family?", an example of which is presented on Figure A.4.

What is necessary to have a family?
Is it better to be one child or have siblings?
Is it more difficult to be the oldest brother/sister or the youngest?
Should a family have rules?
Is it always good to be with family?
Should we trust in our family?
In a family, is everyone treated in the same way?

Figure A.1. *List of questions to be answered individually.*

What is the question for which I have the competence to reply in my role as ....?
Write the question:

What is my answer?
MY ANSWER:

Where do I base my answer?
MY DATA-EVIDENCE FOR THE ANSWER I GAVE:

Figure A.2. *Individual answer template.*

Appendix 119

Group question: WHAT IS FAMILY?

Group answer (Try to integrate as many elements as possible from the group members' answers to the individual questions. You can also integrate evidence from the texts you read to reinforce your definition. Finally you can mark in different colors the contributions of each one of you to the final answer).

We define Family as:

To say this, we were based on different data, such as:

Figure A.3. *Group answer template.*

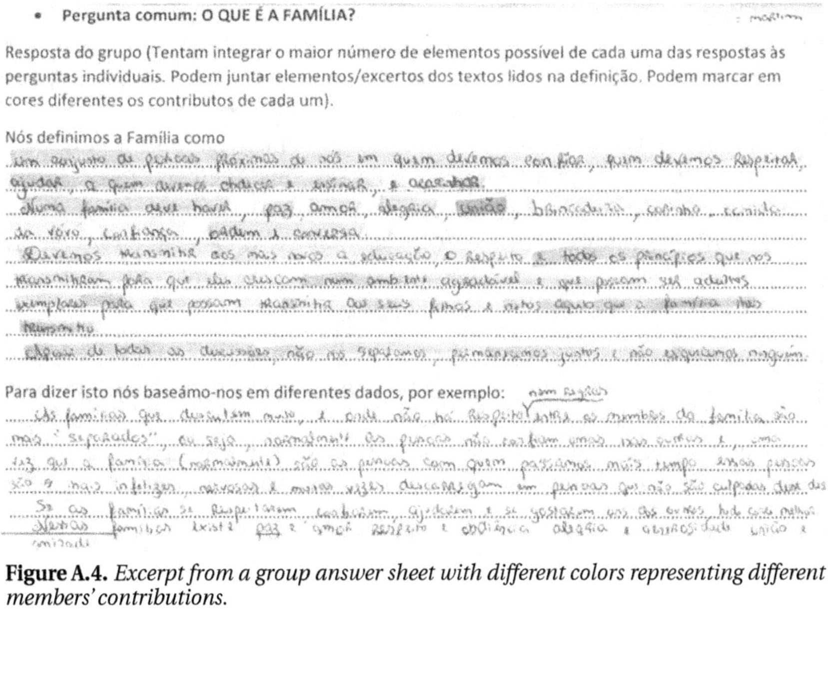

- **Pergunta comum: O QUE É A FAMÍLIA?**

Resposta do grupo (Tentam integrar o maior número de elementos possível de cada uma das respostas às perguntas individuais. Podem juntar elementos/excertos dos textos lidos na definição. Podem marcar em cores diferentes os contributos de cada um).

Nós definimos a Família como

[handwritten response]

Para dizer isto nós baseámo-nos em diferentes dados, por exemplo:

[handwritten response]

Figure A.4. *Excerpt from a group answer sheet with different colors representing different members' contributions.*

Session 2 (90 minutes): The students were given as homework (they had one whole week to prepare) a list of family types created as part of a research project by the University of Coimbra (https://digitalis.uc.pt/en/livro/novos_tipos_de_família_plano_de_cuidados). Their task was to select at least three characteristics that match with their family and explain, preparing a small discourse, why these characteristics were the ones that best described their own families. All students presented their answers to the audience consisting by the class, the teacher, and an expert in argumentation (i.e. the author of this book). All audience members had to secretly rate the presentations in terms of several criteria being given to them by the teacher in the form of a rating scheme. Some of these criteria were: clarity of contents, capacity of expressing and explaining, capacity of arguing, and originality. At the end of the activity the two best presentations were selected, also consulting the expert's opinion about the arguing aspects.

Session 3 (90 minutes). The students were given a shorter list of family characteristics created by the teacher, mostly including adjectives such as: serious, funny, brave, lovely, intelligent, lazy, etc. They were asked to sit in their groups and come up with a decision about which of those characteristics best represented their fictitious group family (already being named in Session 1). This was a bonding activity, preparing for the role-playing decision making activity that followed. Groups were given one scenario each, created by the teacher, requiring a decision to be made by them as a family. The six scenarios were the following: 1) "The holidays are near, where do we go?"; 2) "Our family has to move and we have to choose where to live"; 3) "The mother wants to go back to University, and less money will come home. How will we organize ourselves?"; 4) "It's a family member's birthday and we need to prepare a celebration party"; 5) "There is a relative who wants to stay with our family for a year, how will we organize the everyday life?"; and 6) "One of the family members became unemployed; how can we re-organize our family life?".

Session 4 (90 minutes). All groups represented their "family" decision-making process on the issue of their scenario presented above. They used role-playing to do that, each member adopting the perspective of a family member putting forward his/her needs and values. The representations were examples of everyday practical reasoning situations, involving genuine argumentation, disagreement, and resolution of the disagreement with a final decision, not necessarily baing shared by everyone.

Appendix

Argument-based activity in History

Context

Portuguese 9th grade (age 14-15 years old) class History class. The curricular program starts from Europe in the 19th century, covers the two World Wars and the Russian revolutions, with a special focus on the Portuguese participation in the First World War and its consequences at all levels, as well as the political history of Portugal in the 20th century.

Focus

The focus of the activity is on the Cold War period, between 1947 and 1991, and more precisely on understanding whether the lack of military conflicts during that period could be considered as equivalent to peace.

Structure of the activity

The activity was developed in one session of 45 minutes. The students sat in their groups, selected by them, and were given the work sheet appearing on Figure A.5. Students had to, first individually and then with their groups, express their opinion based on evidence on the following statement "During the Cold War, there were alternately conflict phases and calming stages". The individual reflection part consisted in students writing down weather they agree or not with the statement and justify their answer. In the group activity part, students were invited to compare their answer to the others', try to persuade the members of the group with different views, and in the end decide on a group answer based on the preceding debate. Students could use evidence from their textbook, as well as from the three documents given by the teacher on the top of their work sheet. Document 1 consists of an image and a short text from an internationally recognized source (Eric Hobsbawm); Document 2 is an image representing the Berlin Blockade; Document 3 is a short excerpt from an essay published by Nikita Khrushchev, ex Chairman of the Council of Ministers of the Union of Soviet Socialist Republics.

Doc. 1
A. The two Super Powers

B – *The Cold War*

Though the most obvious face of the Cold War was military confrontation and an ever-more frenetic nuclear arms race in the West, this was not its major impact. The nuclear arms were not used. Nuclear powers engaged in three major wars (but not against each other).

Hobsbawm, E. (1995). Age of Extremes. The Short Twentieth century 1914-1991.

Doc. 2 – Berlin blockade

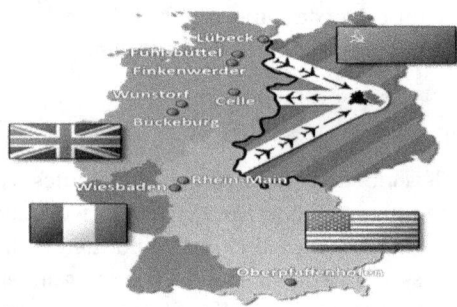

Doc. 3 – *On Peaceful Coexistence,*

Nikita Krushchev (1959)

You may like your neighbor or dislike him. You are not obliged to be friends with him or visit him. But you live side by side, and what can you do if neither you nor he has any desire to quit the old home and move to another town? All the more so in relations between states. It would be unreasonable to assume that you can make it so hot for your undesirable neighbor that he will decide to move to Mars or Venus. And vice versa, of course.

"DURING THE COLD WAR THERE WERE ALTERNATELY CONFLICT PHASES AND CALMING STAGES"	
My opinion	Agree or not
	Reasons
I compare my opinion with that of others	What is the opinion of the other members of your group? In agreement:
	In disagreement:
	Try to give reasons that persuade others to share your opinion:
	Write now the most plausible view of your group:

Figure A.5. *The work template in the History argument-based activity.*

Argument-based activity in Science

Context

Portuguese 9th grade (age 14-15 years old) Natural sciences class. The curricular program covers the following main thematic areas: individual and community health, human reproduction, basic notions of heredity, human physiology and interaction between the human body systems.

Focus

The focus of the activity is on the socio-scientific issue on whether or not the use of cellphones can be dangerous to humans.

Structure of the activity

Students were divided in groups of 5-6. They were given a trigger, which was that the teacher entered the class, took the trash bin, and asked everyone to put their cellphones inside. After a short free, wholeclass interaction regarding whether or not the use of cellphones was really dangerous, she gave each group an argument map (see Figure A.6), that they had to fill in as a group using evidence from three one-page texts, previously selected by the teacher. Text 1 reported on findings regarding the relation between fertility and use of cellphones by men, based on scarce evidence; Text 2 related the use of cellphones with cancer and neurological diseases; whereas Text 3 commented on the uncertainty regarding the findings of studies relating the use of cellphones with cancer, and shifted the attention, instead, to some indirect risks, such as the case of car accidents. Overall, the information included in the texts was often vague and disputable.

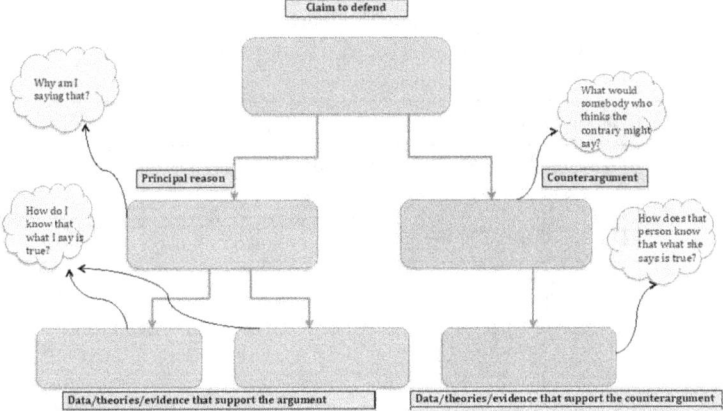

Figure A.6 *The argument map structure.*

Students were asked to evaluate these sources and to argue in favor or against the statement that the use of cellphones is dangerous for humans. As students were already exposed to argument-based teaching before, they were expected to be able to take either part, as the focus was on their capacity to argue and not on what they really believed.

After all groups had completed their maps, the teacher asked individual students to choose their group's strongest argument in favor or against the position, and a "train-form" debate was conducted by volunteers until no more arguments were left to be expressed. The train-form debate refers to a flexible structure of volunteer students divided to two sides of an argument, one in favor, the proposition, and one against, the opposition. Behind the first two students who get up to state either an argument or a counter-argument, a line is formed, like a train, by other volunteer students who come up with more evidence in favor or against. Students take turns to present their arguments, in favor or against, and respond to the other side, trying to persuade the rest of their class one way or the other. The students who do not volunteer to form part of the train participate in two main ways: first, they are free to challenge the spokespeople and to judge whether an argument stated is good enough to be part of the train; second, they conclude the debate by forming balanced arguments integrating the strongest evidence from both parts.

Table A1. **Example of classroom discourse coding using TAP elements (the excerpt was translated from the original language, i.e. Portuguese).**

Speaker	Discourse	Code
S6	(...) I use more energy inside, inside and environment... in a closed environment than outside... when i'm, for example, running in the... [ ]... (teacher interrupts)	refine backing
Teacher	You'd rather do?	
S6	I'd rather do it outside... because i use less energy, i don't know what happens!	warrant
Choir	[ ] (they all speak at the same time)	
Teacher	Is not spending more or less energy, what do you think... no, no, no []	reject warrant

Teacher	ehh... what... in, in... what he's sayin', that he rather do it outside, than in, because, oh... sorry, outdoors then in the gym... because in the gym... he gets more tired! that has to do with what?	invite warrant
S7	air density?	warrant
S8	mine is... the mitocondrias don't have... enough oxygen to... to.. send energy to the muscles, as it has a lot of carbon, so he feels more tired!	warrant
S9	(...) Ok, the pros and cons of spaces... closed spaces there's more bacteria and virus transmission amongst people... and then everyone gets sick if anyone's sick. In the outdoor there's also bacteria and virus, so we can also get sick.	integrative reply
S9	[ ] but, there's more oxygen... than in an indoor place,	rebuttal
S9	as air keeps... it's always the same air and we're breathing it, it's... more carbon doxide out... and then the carbon dioxide concentration starts to increase and that of oxygen decreases...[ ]	backing
S10	it depends... it depends on the existence of windows, are things that...	claim & data
S11	Oh, Tiago, opening a window isn't the same thing as... [ ] being outdoors...	counterargument
S10	if we have... [ ]	
Choir	[ ] (everyone speaks at the same time, including the teacher)	
S10	... [ ] closed space is... can have... if it has holes... [ ] and we can breathe... the air gets in and out... then the closed space is... no one has to die because there's more carbon dioxide... oxygen still gets in, can be... [ ]	backing
Teacher	(chiuuu...chiuuu) what were you sayin'?	
S10	it's... [ ] closed space, if we're making sports in a closed space and that which...half an hour later, start having that feeling that we're in a much... it's... claustrophobic and we're in a prison and... [ ]	refine backing

Table A2. Coding results of all students' texts before and after teacher training.

ID	Pre-training		Post-training		ID	Pre-training		Post-training	
1	CDCAR	2	CDS2CA	4	41	C2D3	1	CII	0
2	CDS3E	3	CDS4E	3	42	C2D2SII	1	CDS	2
3	CDSE	2	CDCA	2	43	C2D2	1	CDCAR	4
4	CDSE	2	E	0	44	C2D2S2	2	CDSE	2
5	CDSCACASR	6	CE	0	45	C2D2	1	CD2CACAS	5
6	CDE	1	CDSE	2	46	C2D2	1	CDS	2
7	CD2S2E	3	CD3S2	3	47	C2D3	1	CD2SCAR	5
8	CDE	1	CDS	2	48	C2D2	1	CDE	1
9	CD2	1	CD2S2	3	49	C2D2	1	CDSCAR	5
10	CD	1	CDSE	2	50	C2D2	1	CD2SCACAS	5
11	CDE3	1	CDII	1	51	CD	1	II	0
12	CD3SE	2	CDSCAR	5	52	CDE	1	CD	1
13	CDEII	1	CDSE	2	53	II	0	CDE	1
14	CDSCA	4	CDS2II	2	54	CD3S2E	3	CDS3CA	4
15	CD4II	1	CD3	1	55	II	0	CDSII	1
16	CDSII	1	CD4SII	1	56	CD5SCAR	5	C2D2S2	3
17	CD2S	2	CD2S2	3	57	CE	0	C2D2S2	3
18	CD2	1	CD2S	2	58	CDE3II	1	CE	0
19	CDS	2	CD2S	2	59	CEIIDS4CA	3	CDEII	1
20	CD4	1	CD	1	60	ECD	1	CD3E	1
21	CD2	1	CD	1	61	E	0	CD3S	2
22	CDE	1	CDS2	3	62	CDS6	3	CD2S2	3
23	CEDII	1	CDS2CA	4	63	CD4CAII	1	CD2E	1
24	CDSE	2	CD3S2E	3	64	CD2S2	3	CD2SE	2
25	CD3	1	CDSCA	4	65	CD5SCACASR	6	CDEII	1
26	CDES	2	CDCACAS2	4	66	CDS2CA	4	CD3S	2
27	CDS	2	CD2S2E	3	67	CDE3	1	CED2S2	3
28	CD2	1	CD3S2E	3	68	CD2S3CA	4	CD2S3	3
29	C2D3S	2	CDS	2	69	CDS2IIE	1	CD3S	2
30	C2D3S2	3	CD3CACAS	4	70	CD2	1	CDE	1
31	C2D3	1	CDE	1	71	II	0	CD2E	1
32	C2D2S	2	CD2II	0	72	CD4S2	3	CD2S	2
33	CD2	1	CDS2II	2	73	CDS4	3	CD3ECACAS	3
34	C2D4S2	3	CDS2CACAS	5	74	CD2CA	2	CD5CA	2
35	C2D3II	1	CD2S2	3	75	CDES	2	CDSCACASRE	6
36	C2D3S3	3	CDE	1	76	CD2CA	2	CD3CACASR	5
37	C2D2S2E	3	CDS	2	77	CD4CA3	2	CDSCACAS2	5
38	C2D3S	2	CDS	2	78	CIID2	1	CDS	2
39	CDE	1	CD2S2CA	4	79	CDES4CA3CAS	5	CDS2CACASR	6
40	CD2	1	CD2	1	80	CDS3	3	CD5ECA	2

Index

A

abductive, 8, 11, 41, 43, 50, 53, 58, 59, 63, 64
abductive reasoning, 8, 41, 43, 50, 53, 58, 63
acceptability, x, 5, 57, 62, 69
accountability
  accountable, 58, 59
Alexander, 7, 40
antilogos, xi, 69, 78
aporia, 37, 41, 42, 43, 45, 49, 50
argument skills, ix, xiii, 1, 4, 30, 36, 68
argument1 type, 6
argument2 type, 6
Argumentation Rating Tool, 7, 73
argumentative discourse, xii, xiv, 1, 2, 4, 6, 7, 8, 11, 13, 18, 30, 35, 36, 67, 70, 76
argument-based teaching, xiii, xiv, xv, 1, 20, 51, 67, 68, 70, 71, 72, 73, 75
authority, 17, 40, 50, 59, 60, 63

B

backing, x, xi, 4, 33, 54, 57, 59, 60, 61, 62, 64, 78, 80
Berland, ix, 2, 15, 20, 21, 22, 23, 24, 25, 28, 29, 31, 33, 36, 41, 68, 91, 94, 105
bias, xi, 69
burden of proof, 50, 57, 61, 62, 63, 64

C

Chinn, 16, 67, 106
claim, ix, x, 4, 6, 17, 28, 32, 33, 34, 35, 40, 53, 54, 55, 56, 59, 60, 61, 63, 64, 68, 69, 77, 78, 80, 89, 90, 91
Claim-Evidence-Reasoning, 91
co-construction, xii, 34, 40, 87
collaboration, 40
counterarguments, xi, xii, xiii, 24, 33, 34, 57, 67, 68, 76, 78, 79, 80, 82, 83
critical argumentation, ix, xv, 68, 69, 70, 71, 73, 76, 77, 78, 79, 80, 83, 85
Critical questioning, xii
critical thinking, 29, 30, 33, 35, 37, 50, 69, 70, 76, 78, 85, 89, 103
Critical thinking, 33, 34

D

data, x, xii, 4, 6, 10, 11, 13, 17, 18, 20, 21, 25, 29, 33, 41, 53, 54, 55, 56, 57, 58, 59, 60, 61, 62, 63, 64, 68, 69, 76, 77, 78, 80, 84, 90, 91, 100
deductive, x, 8, 16, 50, 53, 58, 63
design-based research, 71
dialectical, xi, 16, 41, 43, 44, 50, 102, 109
dialogic teaching, 2, 7, 8, 40, 48, 73
dialogue, xii, xiv, 6, 7, 9, 11, 29, 33, 34, 35, 37, 40, 41, 42, 43, 44, 45, 47, 48, 49, 50, 51, 61, 69, 70, 71,

72, 73, 85, 87, 89, 91, 92, 93, 94, 97, 99, 102, 103
disciplinary fields, xv, 59, 61, 67, 69
discourse moves, 20, 30, 31, 35

E

epistemic, 33, 40, 41, 43, 49, 50, 54, 59, 76, 92, 97, 103
evidence, xi, xii, xiii, 7, 9, 11, 13, 15, 17, 21, 22, 23, 25, 26, 27, 28, 29, 31, 32, 33, 34, 39, 40, 41, 44, 45, 47, 48, 50, 53, 54, 55, 56, 57, 58, 59, 60, 61, 62, 63, 67, 68, 70, 76, 77, 78, 79, 83, 84, 90, 91, 99, 105
explanation, xi, 4, 7, 8, 22, 27, 29, 32, 35, 41, 43, 45, 48, 53, 54, 55, 56, 58, 60, 68, 76, 77, 78, 89
exploratory talk, 31, 34, 40, 93

F

Felton, xiii, 1, 6, 41, 67
field-dependency, 55

G

Govier, x, 90

H

historical claim, 59, 60

I

imaginary addressee, 57, 63
inductive, 8, 11, 50, 53, 58, 59, 63, 64, 76
informal logic, x, 69
inquiry, xi, 7, 8, 9, 11, 15, 17, 22, 25, 27, 29, 37, 38, 39, 40, 41, 42, 43, 44, 45, 48, 50, 60, 70, 73, 74, 91, 93, 97, 103
Inquiry-Response-Evaluation (IRE), 2, 7, 16, 43, 92, 93
instructional design, 1, 2, 20, 36, 72
ID, 2, 3, 4, 21
issue, xii, 11, 22, 30, 34, 36, 38, 41, 42, 43, 48, 50, 55, 57, 74, 78, 79, 82, 83

K

Kuhn, ix, xi, xii, xiii, 1, 6, 15, 17, 57, 60, 67, 68, 69, 76, 77, 78, 90

M

McNeill, ix, xii, 1, 18, 22, 23, 24, 28, 30, 32, 33, 35, 36, 54, 55, 68, 70
modus ponens, 58, 59, 63
Mortimer, 7, 16, 93

N

Nussbaum, xii, 6, 67, 111

O

oral argumentation, 91
Osborne, ix, xii, 2, 6, 15, 17, 18, 22, 24, 27, 30, 31, 33, 34, 36, 41, 44, 67, 69, 70, 78, 106, 107, 111, 112, 114

P

pedagogical content knowledge, 1, 35, 70
prior knowledge, 1, 24, 28, 32, 41, 42
project, xv, 2, 7, 71, 72, 73

Q

question, xi, xii, 4, 7, 16, 20, 24, 25, 26, 27, 30, 38, 39, 42, 47, 48, 51, 53, 55, 57, 63, 74, 79, 82, 87, 88, 90, 91, 92, 93, 96

R

reasoning, ix, x, xi, xiv, 4, 6, 8, 11, 13, 16, 17, 18, 23, 26, 28, 29, 31, 32, 33, 35, 36, 39, 40, 41, 42, 50, 51, 53, 54, 55, 56, 57, 58, 60, 62, 63, 67, 68, 69, 70, 78, 85, 88, 91, 93, 102, 106, 108, 109, 110, 111, 112, 113, 114, 115, 120
relevance, 13, 56, 62, 68, 69, 71, 80
Reznitskaya, 2, 7, 8, 16, 45, 73
rubric, 7, 55, 71, 73, 80

S

Sandoval, 67, 76, 77, 113
Schwarz, ix, xi, 67, 69, 77, 84, 105, 107, 113
science argumentation, 1, 15, 17, 36
scientific claim, 13, 59, 60
socio-scientific, 16, 19, 20, 54, 67, 77, 87, 88, 93

strategies, xiii, xiv, xv, 1, 2, 3, 4, 9, 11, 16, 20, 21, 23, 24, 25, 26, 27, 28, 32, 37, 67, 70, 71, 72, 73, 74, 83, 85
sufficiency, 55, 62, 69

T

TAPping, 53, 69, 107
teacher professional development, 18, 68
teacher's role, 17, 34, 43
techniques, 2, 3, 17, 20, 21, 22, 23, 25, 27, 28, 40, 72
tools, 3, 6, 16, 20, 21, 23, 25, 27, 28, 31, 33, 50, 53, 72
Toulmin, x, xiii, 4, 5, 6, 20, 33, 54, 55, 57, 68, 73, 78
Toulmin's Argument Pattern TAP, 4, 68

W

Walton, xi, 6, 33, 35, 37, 41, 44, 50, 53, 58, 62, 69, 73
warrant, x, 4, 33, 54, 56, 57, 59, 60, 61, 62, 63, 78, 80
warrant-using, 59
written argumentation, xii, xiii, 5, 57, 84, 87, 91

www.ingramcontent.com/pod-product-compliance
Lightning Source LLC
Chambersburg PA
CBHW061844300426
44115CB00013B/2497